12 00

MEDIEVAL RHETORIC

A SELECT BIBLIOGRAPHY

TORONTO MEDIEVAL BIBLIOGRAPHIES 3

General Editor: John Leyerle

Published in Association with
the Centre for Medieval Studies, University of Toronto

JAMES J. MURPHY

Medieval Rhetoric

A SELECT BIBLIOGRAPHY

Second Edition

UNIVERSITY OF TORONTO PRESS
Toronto Buffalo London

© University of Toronto Press 1989
Toronto Buffalo London
Printed in Canada

ISBN 0-8020-5750-0 (cloth)
ISBN 0-0820-6659-3 (paper)

Canadian Cataloguing in Publication Data

Murphy, James J. (James Jerome)
  Medieval rhetoric: a select bibliography

  (Toronto medieval bibliographies; 3)
  2nd ed.
  "Published in association with the Centre for
  Medieval Studies, University of Toronto."
  Includes index.
  ISBN 0-8020-5750-0 (bound). — ISBN 0-8020-6659-3 (pbk.)

  1. Rhetoric, Medieval — Bibliography.   I. University
  of Toronto. Centre for Medieval Studies.
  II. Title.   III. Series.

  Z7004.R5M87 1989   016.808′02′0902   C89-093504-1

Page Design and Phototypesetting by Kevin P. Roddy

For P. Osmund Lewry O.P.
(ob. April 23, 1987)
Amicus, Peritus, Sanctus

General Editor's Preface

The study of the Middle Ages has been developed chiefly within university departments such as English or History. This pattern is increasingly being supplemented by an interdisciplinary approach in which the plan of work is shaped to fit the subject studied. The difference of approach is between Chaucer the English poet and Chaucer the civil servant of London attached to the court of Richard II, a man interested in the Ptolemaic universe and widely read in Latin, French, and Italian. Interdisciplinary programs tend to lead readers into areas relatively unfamiliar to them where critical bibliographies prepared with careful selectivity by an expert are essential. The Centre for Medieval Studies at the University of Toronto takes such an interdisciplinary approach to the Middle Ages, and the need for selective bibliographies has become apparent in our work. The Centre has undertaken to meet this need by sponsoring the Toronto Medieval Bibliographies.

In his valuable guide, *Serial Bibliographies for Medieval Studies,** Richard H. Rouse describes 283 bibliographies; the number is surprisingly large and indicates the considerable effort now being made to provide inclusive lists of items relevant to medieval studies. The total amount in print is already vast; for one unfamiliar with a subject, significant work is difficult to locate and the problem grows worse with each year's output. The reader may well say, like the throng in *Piers Plowman* seeking the way to *Treuthe*, 'This were a wikked way but who-so hadde a gyde' (B.vi.I). The

---

*Publications of the Center for Medieval and Renaissance Studies 3, University of California, Los Angeles (Berkeley and Los Angeles 1969)

Toronto Medieval Bibliographies are meant to be such guides; each title is prepared by an expert and gives directions to important work in the subject.

Each volume gives a list of works selected with three specific aims. One is to aid students who are relatively new to the area of study, for example Medieval Latin Palaeography. Another is to guide more advanced readers in a subject where they have had little formal training, for example Chaucer or Medieval Christian Imagery; and the third is to assist new libraries in forming a basic collection in the subject presented. Individual compilers are given scope to organize a presentation that they judge will best suit their subject and also to make brief critical comments as they think fit. Clarity and usefulness of a volume are preferred over any demand for exact uniformity from one volume to another.

Toronto, December 1988
JL

Contents

Preface to the Second Edition

When the original edition of this work was published in 1971, the systematic study of medieval rhetoric had just begun, and it was still sometimes difficult to persuade book publishers or editors of learned journals that medieval language use was an important subject. Yet the groundwork for serious study had long been laid: Rockinger's collection of dictaminal texts dated from 1863, and Faral's texts of *artes poetriae* had appeared in 1924; Charland's and Caplan's monumental surveys of the *artes praedicandi* came out in 1936, and the landmark article of McKeon (*Speculum*, 1942) had presented a considerable advance over the only survey then available (Baldwin's *Medieval Rhetoric and Poetic*, 1928). Ironically though, the appearance of Curtius' *European Literature and the Latin Middle Ages* in 1956 had the effect of inspiring a rash of studies (more than 50 articles and books) of medieval use of tropes and figures—thus reinforcing the view of many that medieval rhetoric was concerned primarily with *elocutio* (Style).

Now the situation is much changed. The whole history of rhetoric, including its medieval phase, is under intense investigation; there is at least one journal (*Rhetorica*) devoted solely to the history of rhetoric, and the subject now appears regularly in serial bibliographies. Numerous texts and translations from the medieval period have appeared, with more under way. The Louvain series *Typology of Sources of the Western Middle Ages,* for example, has six related works in preparation for publication in 1988 or 1989. Two bibliographic studies have been edited by Horner, and there is now available a newer survey (Murphy's *Rhetoric in the Middle Ages*, 1974).

Even though the subject of medieval rhetoric has now become more respectable and more popular than it was in 1971, the dual purposes of this bibliography remain the same—that is, to identify key works from a wide variety of sources, and to show relationships among these works as far as it is possible for a bibliography to do so. Hence the bibliography is both "select" and "categorized."

Therefore this select bibliography is designed to facilitate the study of the preceptive arts of discourse in Europe from the time of Saint Augustine (c. AD 400) to the re-discovery of complete major classical rhetorical texts in the early fifteenth century (Quintilian's *Institutio oratoria*, 1416; Cicero's *De oratore*, 1422).

The history of medieval rhetoric can only be understood as part of medieval man's efforts to understand the manifold uses of language. Consequently this bibliography includes materials concerning the impact of logic upon rhetoric and grammar, and the relation of grammar to rhetoric. Since any serious study of the subject must proceed in full awareness of the complexity of medieval thinking about language and its uses, an effort has been made to arrange the sections of the bibliography to indicate the relationships between various fields.

In the ancient world the chief preceptive art was rhetoric, which presented advice or principles (*praecepta*) to aid speakers in preparing and delivering their discourses. Grammar, "the art of correct speaking and the interpretation of the poets" (as Quintilian defined it), was regarded as a preliminary to the more important study of the rhetoric which prepared men for active civic affairs. From the rhetorician's point of view, logic was merely a device to be used to construct arguments.

From the time of Saint Augustine and Rabanus Maurus, however, the new Christian culture in the west turned ancient doctrines to new purposes. Not only was rhetoric applied directly to preaching (*ars praedicandi*)—the counterpart of ancient oratory—but by the eleventh century the rise of the *ars dictaminis* showed that Ciceronian rhetorical principles could be applied as well to letter-writing. In the twelfth and thirteenth centuries the grammarians turned again to rhetoric for assistance in framing new treatises dealing with poetry (*ars poetriae*) and rhythmics (*ars rithmica*). Medieval grammar thus became a preceptive art like rhetoric. Meanwhile the university practice of *disputatio* was based on Aristotelian dialectic, but with traces of declamation practices from Roman rhetorical schools; this too deserves study as an influence on medieval habits of writing and speaking.

The student of medieval rhetoric should understand, therefore, that this great variety of authors and works can be viewed as falling into several well-defined streams or currents. While a study of medieval rhetoric thus affords insights into such varied facets of the middle ages as education, literature, religion, and diplomacy—into every sphere, in fact, in which the use of language played a part—this bibliography is also designed to show that any systematic investigation of this heterogeneous field must be undertaken with the knowledge that there are several separate mainstreams of medieval rhetoric:

1 Rhetorical works of the ancient world were used selectively throughout the middle ages.
2 Grammatical works based on Ciceronian rhetoric (e.g. "arts of poetry") were written by and taught by professional grammar teachers beginning in the late twelfth century; our understanding of this fact requires a comprehension of the whole field of the medieval *ars grammatica*.
3 Letter-writing manuals (*artes dictaminis*) derived from Ciceronian rhetoric also play an important role after AD 1087.
4 Preaching manuals (*artes praedicandi*) lay out a new and specialized type of "thematic sermon" beginning about AD 1205.
5 University disputation (*disputatio*) relied primarily on

Aristotle's dialectical works but influenced rhetoric in several ways.

SELECTION OF ITEMS

Each of the items has been selected on the basis of its value in providing an entry to the field of study. First priority was given to primary sources (editions and translations); after them came key secondary works with good explanatory surveys. Where several items give approximately equal treatment to a subject, preference has been given to that single item which has the best footnoting or best bibliography for further study.

THE BASIC LIBRARY

For the convenience of readers wishing to begin a study of medieval rhetoric, the Appendix contains a starting library of basic books and articles. All are available in original editions or reprints.

CONSISTENCY OF ENTRY

Medieval rhetoric involves authors from Western Europe, North Africa, and the Near East over a period of more than a thousand years. Texts and scholarship on the subject reflect this range; and strict consistency of entry form in the face of such complexities would be false to the material and is probably impossible. Consequently, the entries have been given in a way that will be most useful to a reader even if some inconsistency has resulted. Several such inconsistencies should be noted here.

A A considerable number of items appear in uncommon volumes or series. For such items fuller information than normal is given; examples are titles in such series as MIÖG or SBAW, since libraries tend to catalogue only the series, not the contents.

B Names of authors from the classical and medieval periods have been anglicized except where they appear in titles. For works where the editorial language is Latin, names of scholars have been left in the Latin form where this may be helpful to a reader when consulting a catalogue.

C Modern authors or editors whose names are consulted in catalogues are given with first name and middle initial (where known). For some few authors with very common last names, the middle name is given in full as well. Modern authors or editors of articles or short pieces in journals or longer works whose names are not consulted in catalogues are given in the form presented in the item. Where an author appears in both these groups, his name has been given in full form. Some inconsistencies remain. Church names and titles are preserved only where they may be helpful in locating a name in a catalogue.

D Capitalization of most titles has been normalized. Those in Latin or Romance languages have only the first word and proper nouns capitalized, except for titles in French beginning with Le, La, or L', where the following noun has also been capitalized. Those in English have all but minor words capitalized. Titles of journals, learned societies, series, and the like are given in the form usual to scholarship in English.

Abbreviations

AFP	*Archivum fratrum praedicatorum*
AHDLMA	*Archives d'histoire doctrinale et littéraire du moyen âge*
AJP	*American Journal of Philology*
App.	Appendix
CIMAGL	*Cahiers de l'institut du moyen âge Grec et Latin*
CUAPS	Catholic University of America Patristic Studies
EHR	*English Historical Review*
JEH	*The Journal of Ecclesiastical History*
MARS	*Medieval and Renaissance Studies*
Medieval Eloquence	
	James J. Murphy, ed. *Medieval Eloquence: Studies in the Theory and Practice of Medieval Rhetoric.* (University of California Press, 1978).
MAE	Medium AEvum
MGH	Monumenta Germaniae Historiae
MIÖG	*Mitteilungen des Instituts für österreichische Geschichtsforschung* (Note: Through vol. 54 (1942) the title was *Mitteilungen des österreichischen Instituts für Geschichtsforschung*; for vol. 55 (1944) the title was *Mitteilungen des Instituts für Geschichtsforschung und Archivwissenschaft in Wien*; for vol. 56 (1948) and afterwards the title is as given here.)
MS	*Mediaeval Studies*
NS	*The New Scholasticism*
PBA	*Proceedings of the British Academy*

PL *Patrologia Latina,* ed. J.P. Migne

PMLA *Publications of the Modern Language Association of America*

QJS *Quarterly Journal of Speech*

Readings Joseph M. Miller, Michael H. Prosser, and Thomas W. Benson, eds. *Readings in Medieval Rhetoric.* (Indiana University Press, 1973).

Renaissance Eloquence

 James J. Murphy, ed. *Renaissance Eloquence: Studies in the Theory and Practice of Renaissance Rhetoric.* (University of California Press, 1983).

Rhetoric in the Middle Ages

 James J. Murphy. *Rhetoric in the Middle Ages: A History of Rhetorical Theory from Saint Augustine to the Renaissance.* (University of California Press, 1974, 1981).

SBAW Sitzungsberichte der bayerischen Akademie der Wissenschaften

SM *Speech Monographs*

I

Background Studies

This first section lists more than one hundred and fifty background books and articles useful for attaining a general understanding of medieval attitudes toward verbal communication. The basic works of ancient times are a part of this background, of course; in addition, a great number of modern studies have delved into medieval culture, language, and education. All of these areas naturally need attention, but the reader is cautioned that some of this background material is generalized and therefore somewhat remote from the actuality of specific works, authors, and ideas. Since there is no substitute for reading the primary works themselves, some readers may wish to consult such background items only after they have acquainted themselves with individual works listed here and in later sections.

A. General Studies

1

Billanovich, Giuseppe and Carla Maria Monti. "Una nuova fonte per la storia della scuola di grammatica e retorica nell'Italia del Trecento: I. Petrarca, Pietro da Moglio e Pietro da Parma. [Billanovich]. II. Il codice Berkeley, Bancroft Library, f.2 Ms AC 13 c 5 [Monti]." *Italia medioevale e umanistica* 22 (1979): 367-412.

2

Camargo, Martin. "Rhetoric." In *The Seven Liberal Arts in the Middle Ages*. Ed. David Wagner. (Indiana University Press, 1983). Pp. 96-124.

> *Concludes that by 1300 all the developments that characterized medieval rhetoric had either reached maturity or had already expired.*

3

Caplan, Harry. *Of Eloquence: Studies in Ancient and Mediaeval Rhetoric*. Ed. Anne King and Helen North. (Cornell University Press, 1970).

> *Eight previously-published essays and two original essays (on Memoria and on the "Alanus" commentary on the Rhetorica ad Herennium).*

4

Colloque sur rhétorique. Calliope I. Ed. R. Chevallier. (Paris, 1979).

> *Some 29 papers from a congress held in Paris in 1977.*

5

Kennedy, George A. *Classical Rhetoric and Its Christian and Secular Tradition from Ancient to Modern Times*. (University of North Carolina Press, 1980).

> *A survey from Greece in the fifth century B.C. to the Scotland of Hugh Blair in the eighteenth, tracing "classical rhetoric and its tradition by examining the various strands of thought which are woven together in different ways at different times" (p. 3). There are chapters on Greek rhetoric in the middle ages (pp.161-172) and Latin rhetoric for the period (pp.173-194).*

6

Kennedy, George A. *Greek Rhetoric Under Christian Emperors.* (Princeton University Press, 1983).

Discussion of late classical and Byzantine rhetoric up to the Twelfth Century.

7

McKeon, Richard. "Rhetoric in the Middle Ages." *Speculum* 17 (1942): 1-32.

Long a standard, this obscurely-written article will repay (and require) close study. It stresses the relations between grammar, rhetoric, and dialectic at various periods in the middle ages, but tends to overemphasize the influence of dialectic on medieval rhetorical theory.

8

Murphy, James J. *Rhetoric in the Middle Ages: A History of Rhetorical Theory from Saint Augustine to the Renaissance.* (University of California Press, 1974, 1981). Published in Italian as *La retorica nel medioevo.* Trans. Vincenzo Licitra. (Naples, 1983). Published in Spanish as *La Retórica en la Edad Media.* Trans. Guillermo Hirata Vaquera. (Mexico City, 1986).

Described in Reinsma (1980) as "A standard history of medieval rhetoric." This volume provides the most comprehensive survey of medieval rhetoric. Its six main chapters cover: ancient rhetoric; the early middle ages; the medieval survivals of classical traditions; and the three "rhetorical genres" of ars poetriae, ars dictaminis, and ars praedicandi (with an extended summary of the Forma praedicandi *[1322] of Robert of Basevorn). See also Murphy* Three Rhetorical Arts *which prints translations of typical texts from each of the three genres described in this volume.*

9

Paquet, Jacques, and Jozef IJeswijn, eds. *Les universités à la fin du moyen âge: Actes du congrès international de Louvain 26-30 Mai, 1975.* (Louvain University Press, 1978).

B. Bibliographies

10

Cranz, F.E. and P.O. Kristeller. *Catalogus translationum et commentariorum. Mediaeval and Renaissance Latin Translations and Commentaries. Annotated Lists and Guides.* Union Académique Internationale. 4 vols. (Catholic University of America Press, 1960-80).

11

Enos, Richard Leo. "Classical Period." In *Historical Rhetoric: An Annotated Bibliography of Selected Sources in English.* Ed. Winifred Bryan Horner. (Boston, 1980). Pp. 1-41.

12

Faulhaber, Charles B. "Retóricas clásicas y medievales en bibliotecas castellanas." *Ábaco* 4 (1973): 151-300.

> *Seventy-one medieval rhetorical works are among the 256 listed. A second edition is in progress.*

13

Faulhaber, Charles B. "Rhetoric in Medieval Catalonia: The Evidence of the Library Catalogues." In *Studies in Honor of Gustavo Correa.* Ed. Charles Faulhaber et al. Scripta humanistica, 17. (Potomac, Maryland, 1986). Pp. 92-126.

14

Gallick, Susan. "Continuity of the Rhetorical Tradition: Manuscript to Incunabulum." *Manuscripta* 23 (1979): 31-47.

15

Gallick, Susan. "Medieval Rhetorical Arts in England and the Manuscript Traditions." *Manuscripta* 18 (1974): 67-95.

16

Grant, Michael. *Greek and Latin Authors, 800 B.C.-A.D. 1000.* (New York, 1980).

> *Some 376 authors, with biographical and bibliographical notes. Anonymi are also included.*

17
International Medieval Bibliography. (1967-).
> *Originally begun by Robert S. Hoyt (Minnesota) and Peter H. Sawyer (Leeds), this twice-yearly publication is now edited by Richard J. Walsh. It includes an Author Index and a Subject Index which usually carries a number of citations for "Rhetoric."*

18
Kristeller, Paul O. *Latin Manuscript Books before 1600: A List of the Printed Catalogues and Unpublished Inventories of Extant Collections.* New, revised ed. (Fordham University Press, 1960).

19
Kristeller, Paul O. "Rhetoric in Medieval and Renaissance Culture." In *Renaissance Eloquence.* Pp. 1-19.

20
L'Année philologique: Bibliographie critique et analytique de l'antiquité gréco-latine. (Paris, 1928-).
> *Regularly includes section on rhetoric of ancient Greek and Roman writers.*

21
Mahoney, Edward P., ed. *Philosophy and Humanism: Renaissance Essays in Honor of Paul Oskar Kristeller.* (Leiden, 1976).
> *Includes (pp.543-89) a bibliography of Kristeller's works to 1974.*

22
Medioevo Latino: Bolletino bibliografico della cultura europea dal secolo VI al XIII. A cura di Claudio Leonardi. (Spoleto, 1980-).
> *An extremely valuable resource. This massive annual "Appendice bibliografia" to the journal* Studi Medievale *is now organized into five parts: (1) Autori e testi; (2) Fortleben (of ancient authors); (3) Argomenti e discipline (more than 30 sub-topics, including rhetoric, grammar, education, etc.); and (4-5) Miscellanee e congressi. There is extensive cross-referencing, not only by title but by content, including authors cited in both books and articles. The scope of coverage may be*

seen from Volume VII (1986 for the year 1984), which has 7,613 items on 919 pages, including 68 pages of Indices. Many items are annotated.

23

Murphy, James J. "Middle Ages." In *The Present State of Scholarship in Historical and Contemporary Rhetoric.* Ed. Winifred Bryan Horner. (University of Missouri Press, 1983). Pp. 40-74.
    A survey of recent scholarship, followed by a select bibliography (pp. 59-74).

24

Reinsma, Luke M. "Middle Ages." In *Historical Rhetoric: An Annotated Bibliography of Sources in English.* Ed. Winifred Bryan Horner. (Boston, 1980). Pp. 45-108.
    Includes 235 primary and secondary sources, all annotated extensively. Primary sources are listed chronologically, secondary sources alphabetically by author.

25

Reinsma, Luke M. "Rhetoric, Grammar, and Literature in England and Ireland before the Conquest: A Select Bibliography." *Rhetoric Society Quarterly* 8 (1978): 29-48.

26

Rouse, Richard H. *Serial Bibliographies for Medieval Studies.* Publications of the Center for Medieval and Renaissance Studies 3. (University of California Press, 1969).
    This extremely valuable guide presents annotated entries for 283 continuing bibliographies pertaining in whole or in part to medieval studies. Students of medieval rhetoric may be particularly interested in section VIII, Intellectual history, and section IX, Literature and Linguistics.

C. Ancient Rhetoric and Grammar

27

Abbott, W., W.A. Oldfather, and N.V. Canter. *Index in Ciceronis Rhetorica.* (University of Illinois Press, 1969).

28

Aristotle. *Rhetoric of Aristotle.* Trans. Lane Cooper. (New York, 1932). (Reprinted 1960.)

29

Aristotle. *Topica* and *De sophisticis elenchis.* Trans. W.A. Pickard-Cambridge. Vol. 1 of *The Works of Aristotle.* Ed. W.D. Ross. (Oxford, [1949-56]).

> *These two Aristotelian logical works were used extensively as textbooks in dialectic in medieval universities. The* Topica *includes (book VIII) directions on the holding of disputations, while the other work treats ways to combat fallacious arguments.*

30

Baldwin, Charles S. *Ancient Rhetoric and Poetic.* (New York, 1924; rpt. Gloucester, Massachusetts, 1959).

> *While this book is highly schematic and lacks clear explanations of the relations between the various verbal arts, it features summaries of the key rhetorical works of Aristotle, Cicero, and Quintilian.*

31

Cicero, Marcus Tullius. *De inventione, De optimo genere oratorum, Topica.* Trans. Harry M. Hubbell. (Harvard University Press, 1949).

> *Cicero's* De inventione *was known during the middle ages as his "Old Rhetoric" or "First Rhetoric" while the pseudo-Ciceronian* Rhetorica ad Herennium *was called his "New Rhetoric" or "Second Rhetoric"; see Pseudo-Cicero.*

32

Clark, Donald L. *Rhetoric in Greco-Roman Education.* (Columbia University Press, 1957).

> *Clark presents a topical survey of ancient rhetorical concepts*

rather than a chronological history.

33

Clarke, Martin L. *Rhetoric at Rome: A Historical Survey.* (London, 1953).

Clarke's work is the most useful brief analysis of Roman oratory and rhetoric despite the author's admitted prejudice against rhetoric.

34

Donatus, Aelius. *Ars grammatica.* In *Grammatici latini.* Ed. Heinrich Keil. 4 vols. (Leipzig, 1864). Pp. 367-402. (Reprinted Hildesheim, 1981.)

The Ars grammatica *was also known as the* Ars maior *and was a standard elementary text throughout the middle ages. The last of its three books contains an illustrated discussion of tropes and figures and often circulated separately under the title* Barbarismus *(its first word).*

35

Donatus, Aelius. *Donati de partibus orationis: ars minor.* In *Grammatici latini.* Ed. Heinrich Keil. 4 vols. (Leipzig, 1864). Pp. 355-66. (Reprinted Hildesheim, 1981.)

This standard elementary text, circulated extensively throughout the middle ages, outlines the eight basic "parts of speech."

36

Fiske, George C. and Mary Grant. *Cicero's* De oratore *and Horace's* Ars poetica. (University of Wisconsin Press, 1929).

The authors find more than twenty parallels between the De oratore *and the* Ars poetica.

37

Holtz, Louis. "Grammarians et rhéteurs romains en concurrence pour l'enseignement des figures de rhétorique." *La rhétorique à Rome. Colloque des 10-11 décembre 1977.* Paris: Caesarod- unum XIV bis Calliope I. (Paris, 1979).

38

Horace. *Satires, Epistles and Ars poetica.* Ed. and trans. H. Rushton Fairclough. (Harvard University Press, 1955).

Horace's advice to writers of literature in his Ars poetica *demonstrates the close relation between grammar and rhetoric in ancient times. Geoffrey of Vinsauf's thirteenth-century* Poetria nova *is a medieval attempt to write a "new poetics" to replace Horace.*

39

Hubbell, Harry M. *Influence of Isocrates on Cicero, Dionysius, and Aristides.* (Yale University Press, 1913).

This fundamental study describes the relation between Cicero's rhetoric and the theories of the Greek rhetorician Isocrates. It should be read together with Solmsen's description of the contrasting Aristotelian tradition.

40

Julius Victor. *C. Julii Victoris Ars rhetorica.* Ed. R. Giomini and M.S. Celentano. Teubner Series. (Leipzig, 1980).

41

Kennedy, George A. *Art of Persuasion in Greece.* (Princeton University Press, 1963).

This is probably the best single discussion of Greek oratory and rhetoric in English.

42

Kennedy, George A. *Art of Rhetoric in the Roman World, 300 B.C.-A.D. 300.* (Princeton University Press, 1972).

A major survey, with important chapters on both the rhetoric and the oratory of Cicero, on the rhetoric and oratory of the Augustan period, on Quintilian, and on the Second Sophistic.

43

Kennedy, George A. *New Testament Interpretation through Rhetorical Criticism.* (University of North Carolina Press, 1984).

Proposes readings of the New Testament "as it would be read by an early Christian, by an inhabitant of the Greek-speaking world in which rhetoric was the core subject of formal education."

44

Kustas, George L. *Studies in Byzantine Rhetoric.* Analecta Vlata-don 17. (Thessaloniki, 1973).

Six brief but detailed chapters on Hermogenes, Aphthonius and the Neo-platonists, on Greek Christian rhetoric to A.D. 550, and on such concepts as obscurity and emphasis in Greek writers of the period.

45

Lehnert, Georgius, ed. *Declamationes XIX maiores.* (Leipzig, 1905).

These two sets of fictitious declamations, falsely attributed to Quintilian, sometimes appear in medieval library catalogues and thus may mislead the unwary reader into believing that the extremely rare Institutio oratoria *was present in that library.*

46

Martin, Josef. *Antike Rhetorik: Technik und Methode.* Handbuch der Altertumswissenschaft ; Zweite Abteilung, Dritter Teil. (1974).

Systematic, if over-detailed, survey of the technical rhetoric of the ancient world.

47

Murphy, James J. *Synoptic History of Classical Rhetoric.* (Davis, California, 1983).

An overview of ancient Greek and Roman theory, with anno-tated summaries of Aristotle's Rhetoric *(Forbes I. Hill), of Cicero's seven rhetorical works (Donovan J. Ochs), and of Quintilian's* Institutio oratoria *(Prentice A. Meador, Jr.), with historical surveys by the volume editor.*

48

Prosser, Michael W. and Thomas H. Benson, eds. *Readings in Classical Rhetoric.* (Indiana University Press, 1972; rpt. Davis, California, 1988).

49
[Pseudo-Cicero]. *Rhetorica ad Herennium.* Ed. and trans. Harry Caplan. (Harvard University Press, 1954).

> *The* Rhetorica ad Herennium *was generally regarded during the middle ages as Cicero's own work; its lengthy discussion of tropes and figures in book IV became a medieval standard, and this fourth book, frequently re-copied and circulated as a separate work, influenced almost every medieval rhetorical theorist.*

50
Quintilian. *Institutio oratoria.* Trans. H.E. Butler. 4 vols. (Harvard University Press, 1953).

> *Quintilian's* Institutio *(c.AD 95) provides a detailed description of Roman rhetorical pedagogy, especially the role of imitatio. It therefore illustrates the close connection between rhetorical and grammatical training in the way the Roman schools were organized.*

51
Quintilian On the Teaching of Speaking and Writing. Trans. the Reverend John Selby Watson and James J. Murphy, with Introduction by James J. Murphy. (Southern Illinois University Press, 1987).

> *Translations from Books One, Two, and Ten of Quintilian's* Institutio oratoria, *dealing with the systematic educational processes typical of Roman schools. The introduction includes a discussion of Quintilian's influence during the middle ages.*

52
Russell, Donald A. *Criticism in Antiquity.* (University of California Press, 1981).

> *Argues that "the dominant rhetorical element" in ancient criticism is due to a concern for "potential practitioners" who desire prescriptive advice about future compositions.*

53
Scaglione, Aldo. *Classical Theory of Composition from Its Origins to the Present: A Historical Survey.* University of North Carolina

Studies in Comparative Literature, 53. (University of North Carolina Press, 1972).

54

Smith, Robert W. *Art of Rhetoric in Alexandria: Its Theory and Practice in the Ancient World.* (The Hague, 1974).

55

Solmsen, Friedrich. "Aristotelian Tradition in Ancient Rhetoric." *AJP* 62 (1941): 35-50 and 169-90.

> *This justly famous article presents one of the best outlines of the fundamental elements of Aristotle's rhetorical theory. It should be compared with Hubbel's description of the contrasting Isocratean-Ciceronian tradition.*

56

Wartelle, André. *Lexique de la 'Rhétorique' d'Aristote.* (Paris, 1982).

57

Winterbottom, Michael, ed. *Minor Declamations Ascribed to Quintilian.* (Berlin, 1984).

> *Winterbottom's introduction provides useful information about the probable origin of the pseudo-Quintilian declamations in antiquity.*

D. Medieval Culture and Language

58

Abelson, Paul. *Seven Liberal Arts.* (New York, 1906).

> *Still a useful survey despite its age, this work summarizes the basic concept of "liberal arts" and then devotes a chapter each to the history of the trivium of grammar, rhetoric, logic, and the four arts of the quadrivium.*

59

Auerbach, Erich. *Literary Language and Its Public in Late Latin Antiquity and in the Middle Ages.* Trans. Ralph Manheim. Bollingen Series 75. (New York, 1965).

This is a highly perceptive treatment, ranking with that of Curtius as a general introduction to communication in the middle ages.

60

Baldwin, Charles S. *Medieval Rhetoric and Poetic.* (New York, 1928).
There are useful summaries of some medieval treatises, but Baldwin pays little attention to developments in rhetoric after the thirteenth century and tends to stress unduly the role of logic as an influence on medieval rhetoric. The "Poetic" in the title is largely Chaucerian criticism.

61

Bocheński, Innocent M. *History of Formal Logic.* Trans. Ivo Thomas. (University of Notre Dame Press, 1961).

62

Boehner, Philotheus. *Medieval Logic: An Outline of Its Development from 1250 to c.1400.* (Chicago, 1952).

63

Bolgar, Robert R. *Classical Heritage and Its Beneficiaries.* (Cambridge University Press, 1954).
This extremely useful work has numerous citations.

64

Bolgar, R.R., ed. *Classical Influences on European Culture, A. D. 500-1500.* Proceedings of an International Conference Held at King's College, Cambridge, April, 1969. (Cambridge University Press, 1971).

65

Cambridge History of Later Medieval Philosophy: from the Rediscovery of Aristotle to the Disintegration of Scholasticism, 1100-1600. Ed. Norman Kretzmann, A. Kenny, Jan Pinborg, and Eleonore Stump. (Cambridge University Press, 1982).

66

Chaytor, Henry J. *From Script to Print.* (Cambridge University Press, 1945).
Chaytor presents readable general discussions of manuscript

production and printing, and their effect on readers.

67

Clanchy, M.T. *From Memory to Written Record, England 1066-1307.* (London, 1979).

68

Colish, Marcia L. *Mirror of Language: A Study in the Medieval Theory of Knowledge.* (Yale University Press, 1968). (Reprinted Revised Edition: University of Nebraska, 1983.)

> *The Preface (p. ix) states that "This book treats four medieval thinkers—Augustine, Anselm, Aquinas, Dante—as exponents of a common conception of words as signs in a theory developed by Augustine and expressed by him and his successors in the modes of the Trivium." The discussions of the "rhetorical poetic" of Dante and the "linguistic epistemology" of Augustine may be of particular interest to historians of rhetoric.*

69

Curtius, Ernst R. *European Literature and the Latin Middle Ages.* Trans. Willard R. Trask. Bollingen Series 36. (New York, 1953).

> *This is a provocative treatment of a wide variety of literary and rhetorical topics, especially metaphor and topoi. Not intended as a survey history, it stresses the author's critical comparisons of ancient and medieval authors, themes, and stylistic patterns. Indispensable.*

70

de Bruyne, Edgar. *Esthetics of the Middle Ages.* Trans. Eileen B. Hennessy. (New York, 1969).

> *This excellent survey was originally published in French as Études d'ésthétique médiévale (Geneva, 1975); volume two begins with a discussion of the rhetorical genres of ars dictaminis, ars poetriae, and ars praedicandi.*

71

de Ghellinck, Joseph. *Le Mouvement théologique du XIIᵉ siècle.* 2nd ed. (Bruges, 1948).

> *Despite its title, this volume includes a useful discussion of medieval cultural patterns helpful in interpreting later*

rhetorical developments.

72
Farrar, Clarissa P., and Austin P. Evans. *Bibliography of English Translations from Medieval Sources.* Columbia University Records of Civilization 39. (Columbia University Press, 1946).

73
Fink-Errera, Guy. "La produzione dei libri di testo nelle università medievali." In *Libri e lettori nel Medioevo: Guida storica e critica.* A cura di G. Cavallo. Vol. 419. (Rome, 1977). Pp. 133-165 and 284-302.

74
Gaur, Albertine. *History of Writing.* (London, 1984).

75
Haskins, Charles H. *Renaissance of the Twelfth Century.* (Harvard University Press, 1927).
> *This extremely influential volume (now reprinted: Meridian Books no. 49, 1957) details the short-lived "revival" of classical lore in twelfth-century Europe, especially France.*

76
Haskins, Charles H. "Spread of Ideas in the Middle Ages." *Speculum* I (1926): 19-30.
> *Haskins argues that medieval ideas, rather than being static, tended to be spread throughout Europe by travelers.*

77
Koch, Joseph. *Artes liberales von der antiken Bildung zur Wissenschaft des Mittelalters.* (Leiden, 1959).

78
Labriolle, Pierre de. *Histoire de la littérature latine chrétienne.* 2 vols. 3rd ed. (Paris, 1947).

79
Lehmann, Paul, and Paul Ruf. *Mittelalterliche Bibliothekskataloge Deutschlands und der Schweiz.* 3 vols. (Munich, 1918-62).

80

Lough, John. *Writer and Public in France: From the Middle Ages to the Present Day.* (Oxford, 1978).

81

Manitius, Max. *Geschichte der lateinischen Literatur des Mittelalters.* 3 vols. (Munich, 1911-31).

This reliable standard survey of the subject to the beginning of the thirteenth century contains a large number of references to works dealing with rhetoric, grammar, and dialectic. These subjects themselves are not adequately indexed for the reader, however, and must be located through knowledge of authors' names. Each volume covers a chronological period, with sections on the trivium *and other aspects of language.*

82

Manitius, Max. *Handschriften antiker Autoren in mittelalterlichen Bibliothekskatalogen.* Ed. Karl Manitius. (Leipzig, 1935).

This provides an important summary of medieval library catalogue listings of classical and medieval authors, including their dates of record.

83

Meyer, Otto, with Renate Neumullers-Klauser. *Clavis mediaevalis: Kleines Wörterbuch der Mittelalterforschung.* (Wiesbaden, 1966).

This is a dictionary of medieval terms.

84

Michel, Alain. *La parole et la beauté: rhétorique et esthétique dans la tradition occidentale.* Collection d'études anciennes publiée sous le patronage de l'Association Guillaume Budé. (Paris, 1982).

Although the sections devoted specifically to the middle ages (pp. 139-186) are comparatively brief, this sensitive analysis is well worth examination.

85

Murdoch, J.E. and E.D. Sylla, eds. *Cultural Context of Medieval Learning.* Proceedings of the First International Colloquium on Philosophy, Science, and Theology in the Middle Ages, September

1973. (Dordrecht, 1975).

86

Norden, Eduard. *Die antike Kunstprosa vom VI. Jahrhundert v. Chr. bis in die Zeit der Renaissance.* 2 vols. 5th ed. (Stuttgart, 1958).

> *A key survey of stylistic theories from Gorgias to the Renaissance humanists, this basic work should be studied by any serious student of medieval language or its uses.*

87

Paré, G., A. Brunet, and P. Tremblay. *La Renaissance du XIIe siècle: les écoles et l'enseignement.* Publications de l'institut d'études médiévales d'Ottawa, 3. (Paris, 1933).

88

Poole, Reginald L. *Illustrations of the History of Medieval Thought and Learning.* (London, 1920).

89

Raby, Frederic J.E. *History of Christian-Latin Poetry from the Beginnings to the Close of the Middle Ages.* 2nd ed. (Oxford, 1953).

90

Rand, Edward K. *Founders of the Middle Ages.* (Harvard University Press, 1928). (Reprinted New York, 1957.)

91

Sandys, John E. *History of Classical Scholarship, vol. I: From the Sixth Century B.C. to the End of the Middle Ages; vol. II: From the Revival of Learning to the End of the Eighteenth Century.* 3rd ed. (New York, 1964).

> *While often inaccurate in detail, this book when used with caution can provide general outlines of periods, movements, and data on individual authors. Each chapter is preceded by a chronological table. Volume II includes the fourteenth century in Italy.*

92

Sandys, John E., ed. *Companion to Latin Studies.* 3rd ed. (Cambridge University Press, 1925).

93

Taylor, Henry O. *Classical Heritage of the Middle Ages.* (New York, 1901; rpt. 1929 and 1957).

94

Taylor, Henry O. *Mediaeval Mind.* 2 vols. 4th ed. (Harvard University Press, 1949).

> *Taylor's readable discussions of such general topics as chivalry and intellectual life are crammed with interesting details giving the flavor of the times.*

95

Thompson, James W. *Literacy of the Laity in the Middle Ages.* University of California Publications in Education, IX. (University of California Press, 1939).

96

Wallach, Leopold, ed. *Classical Tradition: Literary and Historical Studies in Honor of Harry Caplan.* (Cornell University Press, 1966).

97

Wulf, Maurice de. *Histoire de la philosophie médiévale.* 3 vols. 6th ed. (Louvain, 1934-7).

> *Two partial translations of this edition were made by Ernest C. Messenger under the title* History of Mediaeval Philosophy *1 and 2 (London [1935-8]) and 1 (London [1951], New York [1952]).*

E. Education

98

Anstey, Henry, ed. *Munimenta academica, or Documents Illustrative of Academical Life and Studies at Oxford.* Roll Series 50. 2 vols. (London, 1868).

99

Billanovich, Giuseppe. "L'insegnamento della grammatica e della retorica nelle università italiane tra Petrarca e Guarino." In *The*

Universities in the Late Middle Ages. Mediaevalia Lovanensia. Series I Studia VI. (Leuven University Press, 1978). Pp. 365-380.

100

Bolgar, Robert R. "Teaching of Rhetoric in the Middle Ages." In *Rhetoric Revalued: Papers from the International Society for the History of Rhetoric.* Ed. Brian Vickers. (Binghamton, New York, 1982). Pp. 79-86.

101

Brooks, Nicholas, ed. *Latin and the Vernacular Languages in Early Medieval Britain.* (Leicester University Press, 1982).
> *Includes essays (pp.99-165) by Michael Lapidge and R. I. Page on the methods used to study Latin texts in late Anglo-Saxon England.*

102

Catto, Jeremy I., ed. *Early Oxford Schools.* Vol. 1 of *The History of the University of Oxford.* Ed. T.H. Aston. (Oxford, 1984).
> *P. Osmund Lewry notes (p.431) that at Oxford "Rhetoric was the neglected member of the* Trivium.*"*

103

Chapman, Janet A. "'I lerned never rethoryk': A Problem of Apprenticeship." In *Medieval Hispanic Studies Presented to Rita Hamilton.* Ed. A.D. Deyermond. (London, 1976). Pp. 21-30.
> *Deals with Juan Ruiz's education.*

104

Clerval, J. Alexandre. *Les écoles de Chartres au moyen-âge du Ve au XVIe siècle* (Paris, 1895).
> *This is an early but still useful treatment of Chartres, an influential center of rhetorical and literary training during much of the middle ages.*

105

Cobban, A.B. *Medieval Universities: Their Development and Organization.* (London, 1975).
> *A major study, with perceptive analyses of the varied forces affecting medieval universities.*

106
Contreni, John J. *Cathedral School of Laon from 850 to 930: Its Manuscripts and Masters.* Münchener Beiträge zur Mediävistik und Renaissance-Forschung, 29. (Munich, 1978).

107
Corbett, James A. *De instructione puerorum of William of Tournai, OP.* Texts and Studies in the History of Mediaeval Education 3. (University of Notre Dame Press, 1955).

108
Courtenay, William J. *Schools and Scholars in Fourteenth-Century England.* (Princeton University Press, 1988).

109
Dainton, C. "Medieval Schools of England." *History Today* 29 (1979): 489-96.

110
Daly, Lowrie J. *Medieval University, 1200-1400.* (New York, 1961).

> This is a popular description of university structure, life, and curriculum, not intended to be as comprehensive as Leff or Rashdall. Since it is rather generalized, its conclusions should be carefully examined.

111
Delhaye, Philippe. "'Grammatica' et 'Ethica' au XIIᵉ siècle." *Récherches de théologie ancienne et médiévale* 25 (1958): 59-110.

> Despite its title, this is most interesting for its treatment of the way medieval educators tried to organize the reading of "authors."

112
Delhaye, Philippe. "L'Organisation scolaire au XIIᵉ siècle." *Traditio* 5 (1947): 211-68.

> This is a detailed account of methods and processes of medieval education.

113
Delisle, Léopold. "Les écoles d'Orléans au douzième et au treizième siècle." *Annuaire-Bulletin de la société de l'histoire de*

France 7 (1869): 139-54.
Although the articles of Léopold Delisle are today very difficult to obtain, almost any one of his closely written studies will repay the effort. This is a fundamental monograph written early in his career.

114
Demnard, D. et D. Fourment. *Dictionnaire d'histoire de l'enseignement.* (Paris, 1981).

115
Denifle, Henricus, and Aemilius Chatelain, eds. *Chartularium universitatis Parisiensis.* 4 vols. (Paris, 1889-97).
This work provides texts of basic university documents to AD 1452.

116
D'Irsay, Stephen. *Histoire des universités françaises et étrangères des origines à nos jours.* 2 vols. (Paris, 1933-5).

117
Drane, Augusta Theodosia (Mother Francis Raphael). *Christian Schools and Scholars.* Ed. Walter Grumbley. 3rd ed. (New York, 1924).

118
Ehlers, J. "Die hohen Schulen." In *Die Renaissance der Wissenschaften im 12. Jahrhundert. Interdisziplinäre Vortragsreihe der Universität Zürich und der Eidgenossische Technische Hochschule. Zürich, Winter 1979-80.* Ed. P. Weimar. (Zürich, 1981). Pp. 57-85.

119
Facchetti, V. "Il 'De magistro' di Tommaso d'Aquino e l'odierna problematica pedagogica." Vol. VIII of *Tommaso d'Aquinas nel suo settimo centenario. Atti del Congresso internazionale, Roma-Napoli, 17-24 aprile, 1974.* (Naples, 1978).

120
Ferruolo, Stephen. *Origins of the University: The Schools of Paris and Their Critics, 1100-1215.* (Stanford University Press, 1985).

121
Fuhrmann, Manfred. *Das systematische Lehrbuch: Ein Beitrag zur Geschichte der Wissenschaften in der Antike.* (Göttingen, 1960).

122
Gabriel, Astrik L. *Garlandia: Studies in the History of the Mediaeval University.* (Frankfurt am Main, Mediaeval Institute of the University of Notre Dame, 1969).

123
Gabriel, Astrik L. *Student Life in Ave Maria College, Mediaeval Paris.* Notre Dame Publications in Mediaeval Studies 14. (University of Notre Dame Press, 1956).

124
Gibson, Strickland, ed. *Statuta antiqua universitatis Oxoniensis.* (Oxford, 1931).

> *These Latin texts provide a good background for understanding medieval Oxford.*

125
Glorieux, Palémon. *Aux origines de la Sorbonne.* I: *Robert de Sorbon* II: *Le Cartulaire.* Vol. 1. Études de philosophie médiévale 53-54 (1966). (Paris, 1965-).

126
Haarhoff, Theodore J. *Schools of Gaul: A Study of Pagan and Christian Education in the Last Century of the Western Empire.* (Oxford, 1920).

> *This is an important source for study of the transition from pagan to Christian education in the West, with special emphasis on the role played by the Roman rhetorical schools of the late Empire.*

127
Hepple, Richard B. *Mediaeval Education in England.* Historical Association Leaflet no. 90. (London, 1932).

> *Hepple offers a brief but comprehensive outline of various types of medieval schools.*

128
Hjort, G. "Theological Schools in Medieval England." *Church Quarterly Review* 116 (1933): 201-18.

129
Hugh of St. Victor. *Didascalicon*. Ed. C.H. Buttimer. (Washington, 1939).

130
Hugh of St. Victor. *Didascalicon of Hugh of St. Victor: A Medieval Guide to the Arts*. Trans. Jerome Taylor. (Columbia University Press, 1961).
> *This is a rare case in which the translator's excellent notes are as valuable as the text they annotate.*

131
Jaeger, Werner. *Early Christianity and Greek Paideia*. (Harvard University Press, 1961).

132
Kibre, Pearl. *Nations in the Mediaeval Universities*. (Cambridge, Massachusetts, 1948).
> *A good bibliography on medieval universities is included.*

133
Leach, Arthur F. *Educational Charters and Documents, 598 to 1909*. (Cambridge University Press, 1911).
> *This excellent collection includes both Latin texts and English translations of key documents. Compare with Thorndike (1944).*

134
Leach, Arthur F. *Schools of Medieval England*. (New York, 1915).
> *Leach's studies of lower schools (i.e. non-university institutions) are still valuable after seven decades.*

135
Leff, Gordon. *Paris and Oxford Universities in the Thirteenth and Fourteenth Centuries: An Institutional and Intellectual History*. (New York, 1968).
> *This is by far the best single brief exposition in English of*

medieval university life, especially the northern institutions like Paris and Oxford. Its readable style and wealth of detail make it an excellent introduction to the subject.

136

Lutz, Cora. *Schoolmasters of the Tenth Century.* (Hamden, Connecticut, 1977).

137

MacKinney, Loren C. *Bishop Fulbert and Education at the School of Chartres.* Notre Dame Texts and Studies in the History of Mediaeval Education 6. (University of Notre Dame Press, 1957).

138

Maierù, Alfonso. "Tecniche d'insegnamento." In *Le scuole degli ordini mendicanti (secoli XIII-XIV).* (Accademia Tudertina Todi, 1978). Pp. 305-352.

139

Maître, Léon. *Les Écoles épiscopales et monastiques en occident avant les universités (768-1180).* 2nd ed. (Paris, 1924).

140

Mallet, Charles E. *Mediaeval University.* Vol. I. A History of the University of Oxford. (London, 1924).

This study, while still somewhat interesting, has long since been surpassed by Cobban, Leff, and Rashdall.

141

Mariétan, Joseph. *Problème de la classification des sciences d'Aristote à St-Thomas.* (Paris, 1901).

Mariétan discusses medieval theories of the interrelation between the various arts and sciences up to the middle of the thirteenth century.

142

McCarthy, J.M. *Humanistic Emphases in the Educational Thought of Vincent of Beauvais.* Studien und Texte zur Geistesgeschichte des Mittelalters, 10. (Leiden, 1976).

143
McMahon, Clara P. *Education in Fifteenth-Century England.* Vol. 35. Johns Hopkins University Studies in Education 35. (Baltimore, 1947).

McMahon presents a useful summary of both university and non-university schooling as well as "class education" for guild apprentices and the like.

144
Moran, Jo Ann Hoeppner. *Growth of English Schooling, 1340-1548: Learning, Literacy and Laicization in Pre-Reformation York Diocese.* (Princeton University Press, 1985).

This meticulous case study of one diocese in northern England includes detailed discussions of literacy and of methods used to teach language use.

145
Mullinger, J. Bass. *History of the University of Cambridge.* (London, 1888).

While deficient in many important respects, Mullinger is still valuable because Cambridge has not received as much recent scholarly attention as Oxford.

146
Murphy, James J. "Literary Implications of Instruction in the Verbal Arts in Fourteenth-Century England." *Leeds Studies in English* NS 1 (1967): 119-35.

This includes a list of identifiable medieval English lower schools (i.e. non-university institutions).

147
Murphy, James J. "Teaching of Latin as a Second Language in the Twelfth Century." *Historiographia Linguistica* 7 (1980): 159-175.

Argues for the continuity of Roman teaching methods such as progymnasmatic exercises and imitatio.

148
Orme, Nicholas. *Education and Society in Medieval and Renaissance England.* (London, 1988).

149

Orme, Nicholas. *Education in the West of England, 1066-1548.* (University of Exeter, 1976).

150

Orme, Nicholas. *English Schools in the Middle Ages.* (London, 1973).

> *An excellent survey which includes a chapter on the teaching of grammar (pp. 87-115) and an Appendix (pp. 293-325) listing some 253 schools known to have existed at various times between 1066 and 1530.*

151

Orme, Nicholas. *From Childhood to Chivalry: The Education of English Kings and Aristocracy 1066-1530.* (London, 1984).

152

Orme, Nicholas. "Grammatical Miscellany of 1427-1465 from Bristol and Wiltshire." *Traditio* 38 (1982): 301-326.

> *Analyzes Lincoln College, Oxford, Manuscript Lat. 129(E) to show how much can be learned about later medieval education from such collections.*

153

Paetow, Louis J. *Arts Course at Medieval Universities with Special Reference to Grammar and Rhetoric.* (Champaign, Illinois, 1910).

> *This classic treatment is indispensable to any study of the trivium of grammar, rhetoric, and logic. While Paetow overestimates the importance of the* ars dictaminis *(he relies heavily on Italian sources), he does provide a clear-cut introduction to his subject.*

154

Parias, L.-H. *Histoire générale de l'enseignement et de l'éducation en France, I: Des origines à la Renaissance.* (Paris, 1983).

155

Pirenne, Henri. "De l'état de l'instruction des laïques à l'époque mérovingienne." *Revue bénédictine* 46 (1934): 165-77.

156
Poole, Reginald L. "Masters of the Schools at Paris and Chartres in John of Salisbury's Time." *EHR* 35 (1920): 321-42.

157
Post, Gaines. "Alexander III, the *Licentia docendi* and the Rise of the Universities." In *Anniversary Essays in Mediaeval History by Students of Charles Homer Haskins.* Ed. C.H. Taylor and J.L. La Monte. (Boston, 1929). Pp. 255-77.

158
Potter, G.R. "Education in the Fourteenth and Fifteenth Centuries." In *Cambridge Medieval History.* Vol. 8. (Cambridge, 1936). Pp. 688-717.
   Despite its prestigious position in the CMH, *Potter's survey is not always reliable when discussing grammar and rhetoric.*

159
Rashdall, Hastings. *Universities of Europe in the Middle Ages.* Ed. F.M. Powicke and A.B. Emden. 3 vols. (Oxford University Press, 1936).
   Rashdall is still the most comprehensive survey of the universities and is indispensable to any serious study of medieval education. There is heavy emphasis on the administrative history of each major institution studied, but curricular and intellectual aspects also receive attention. Documentation provides good resource material for further study in the area covered.

160
Reiche, Rainer. *Ein rheinisches Schulbuch aus dem 11. Jahrhundert. Studien zur Sammelhandschrift Bonn UB.S 218.* Münchener Beiträge zur Mediävistik und Renaissance-Forschung, 24. (München, 1976).
   Includes an edition of the text.

161
Riché, Pierre. "Apprendre à lire et à écrire dans le haut Moyen Âge." *Bulletin de la Société nationale des antiquaires de France* 76 (1978-79): 139-203.

162

Riché, Pierre. *Education and Culture in the Barbarian West, Sixth through Eighth Centuries.* (University of South Carolina Press, 1976).

> *Translation of third edition of* Education et culture dans l'Occident barbare, vi^e^-viiie siècles *(Paris, 1972), an extremely important survey.*

163

Riché, Pierre. *Les écoles et l'enseignement dans l'Occident chrétien de la fin du Ve siècle au milieu du XIe siècle.* (Paris, 1979).

> *A major study of schools, teaching methods, and libraries. Includes chronological tables and a bibliography.*

164

Robson, John A. *Wyclif and the Oxford Schools.* (Cambridge University Press, 1961).

> *This is a perceptive analysis of Lollard thought in the late fourteenth century, providing an interesting view of university life in Chaucer's time.*

165

Smith, Cyril Eugene. *University of Toulouse in the Middle Ages: Its Origins and Growth to 1500 AD.* (Marquette University Press, 1958).

166

Thompson, Alexander H. *Song-Schools in the Middle Ages.* (London, 1942).

> *The "song school" was usually an elementary-level training center for choir members, rather than a "grammar school" which taught language skills.*

167

Thorndike, Lynn. "Elementary and Secondary Education in the Middle Ages." *Speculum* 15 (1940): 400-8.

> *Thorndike stresses the ubiquity of lower schools, arguing that a "supporting network" must have been in existence as feeders to the universities.*

168
Thorndike, Lynn. *University Records and Life in the Middle Ages.* (Columbia University Press, 1944).
This is a good collection of primary source materials, with English translations.

169
Verger, Jacques. *Les universités au Moyen Âge.* (Paris: Presses Universitaires de France, 1973).

170
Verger, Jacques. "Universités et écoles mediévales de la fin du XIe à la fin du XVe siècle." In *Histoire mondiale de l'éducation I: Des origines à 1515.* Ed. G. Mialaret and J. Vial. (Paris: Presses Universitaires de France, 1981).

171
Watson, Foster. *English Grammar Schools to 1660: Their Curriculum and Practice.* (Cambridge University Press, 1908).
Watson emphasizes the differences between medieval and Renaissance schools in their attitudes toward rhetoric.

172
Weijers, Olga. "Collège, une institution avant la lettre." *Vivarium* 21 (1983): 73-82.
Argues that the term "college" was not used before about 1250; other terms were conventus, domus, *until Robert de Sorbon introduced the concept of a secular* collegium.

173
Weisheipl, James A. O.P. "Developments in the Arts Curriculum at Oxford in the Early Fourteenth Century." *MS* 28 (1966): 151-175.

174
Weisheipl, James A. O.P. "Place of the Liberal Arts in the University Curriculum during the XIVth and XVth Centuries." In *Arts libéraux et philosophie au Moyen Age.* (Montréal, Paris, 1969). Pp. 209-213.

175

Wieruszowski, Helene. "Rhetoric and the Classics in Italian Education of the Thirteenth Century." *Studia Gratiana* 11 (1967): 169-207. (Reprinted in her *Politics and Culture in Medieval Spain and Italy*. Rome: Edizioni di Storia e Letteratura, 1971. Pp. 589-627.)

> *Demonstrates that classical poets were studied even in places like Bologna where the* ars dictaminis *was dominant, and that the "vulgarization" of some texts made such studies important to civic life in communes.*

176

Williams, John R. "Cathedral School of Rheims in the Eleventh Century." *Speculum* 29 (1954): 661-77.

II
Early Middle Ages

The period from about AD 400 to the second half of the eleventh century was one in which the dominant force in Europe changed from a Roman civilization, largely pagan, to a feudalism at least nominally Christian. The prime figure in the early rhetorical history of this period is Augustine of Hippo, whose *De doctrina christiana* (completed 426) gave powerful official sanction to the Christian use of Ciceronian rhetoric. During the turmoil of barbarian invasions a number of encyclopedists, compendium writers, and grammarians strove to preserve the rudiments of the ancient arts of discourse. Cicero is the acknowledged rhetorician for these writers. It is noteworthy that the final work of this period is merely a compendium of Ciceronian rhetoric compiled by a German, Notker Labeo, about 1050.

Since many later medieval scholars took their basic concepts of rhetoric and grammar from men like Isidore, Cassiodorus, or Boethius, however, it is vitally important that a modern reader understand how these transitional writers transmitted their ideas.

A. General Studies

177

Bardy, Gustave. "L'Eglise et l'enseignement pendant les trois premiers siècles." *Revue des sciences religieuses* 12 (1932): 1-28.

178

Bardy, Gustave. "Lettrés chrétiens et civilisation romaine à l'aube du moyen âge." *L'Année théologique* 3 (1942): 424-62.

179

Billanovich, Guido. "La lettera di Enrico a Stefano: altri classici a Pomposa (ca.1093)." In *Miscellanea Augusto Campana*. (Padua, 1981). Vol. I. Pp. 141-165.

> *Quintilian and Cicero's* De Oratore *are named in a letter about MSS. acquired or copied by Abbot Giralomo.*

180

Boüard, Michel de. "Encyclopédies médiévales sur la 'connaissance de la nature et du monde' au moyen âge." *Revue des questions historiques* 12 (1930): 258-304.

181

Burns, Sister Mary Albania. *St. John Chrysostom's Homilies on the Statues: A Study of Their Rhetorical Qualities and Form.* CUAPS 22. (Catholic University of America Press, 1930).

182

Buttell, Sister Mary Frances. *Rhetoric of St. Hilary of Poiters.* CUAPS 38. (Catholic University of America Press, 1933).

183

Campbell, James Marshall. *Influence of the Second Sophistic on the Style of the Sermons of St. Basil the Great.* CUAPS 2. (Catholic University of America Press, 1922).

184

Duckett, Eleanor S. *Latin Writers of the Fifth Century.* (New York, 1930).

> *This volume includes numerous quotations from the Christian writers, thus providing valuable background for understanding the fourth century debate over the value of pagan learning.*

185
Ellspermann, Gerard L. *Attitude of the Early Christian Latin Writers toward Pagan Literature and Learning.* CUAPS 82. (Catholic University of America Press, 1949).

186
Evans, Gillian R. "St. Anselm's Technical Terms of Rhetoric." *Latomus* 36 (1977): 171-79.

187
Freni, R. Rallo. "'Divisio' e 'partitio' da Cicerone e Quintiliano a Boezio, Cassiodoro ed Ennodio." *Sileno* 3 (1977): 269-74.

188
Guignet, Marcel. *Saint Grégoire de Nazianze et la rhétorique.* (Paris, 1911).

189
Hagendahl, Harald. *Latin Fathers and the Classics: A Study on the Apologists, Jerome and Other Christian Writers.* (Göteborg, 1958).
> *Hagendahl presents a useful sketch of intellectual currents in the first few Christian centuries.*

190
Jones, Leslie Webber. "Art of Writing at Tours from 1000 to 1200 A.D." *Speculum* 15 (1940): 286-98.

191
Jones, Leslie Webber. "Scriptorium at Corbie, I: The Library." *Speculum* 22 (1947): 191-204.

192
Jurovics, Raachel. "*Sermo Lupi* and the Moral Purpose of Rhetoric." In *The Old English Homily and Its Backgrounds.* Ed. Paul E. Szarmach and Bernard F. Huppé. (State University of New York Press, 1978). Pp. 203-220.

193
Labriolle, Pierre de. *La Réaction païenne: étude sur la polémique antichrétienne du Ier au VIe siècle.* nouvelle édition. (Paris, 1948).

194

Laistner, Max L. W. *Intellectual Heritage of the Early Middle Ages.* (Cornell University Press, 1957).

195

Levison, Wilhelm. *England and the Continent in the Eighth Century.* (Oxford, 1946).

196

McNally, Robert E. *The Bible in the Early Middle Ages.* Woodstock Papers 4. (Westminster, Maryland, 1959).

McNally provides an excellent brief introduction to this subject, with chapters on exegesis, allegory, philology, and other key topics important to an understanding of the relation between biblical studies and medieval attitudes toward communication.

197

Meyer, Robert T. "Old Irish Rhetorical Terms in the Milan Glosses." *Word* 28 (1977 for 1972): 110-116.

Discusses Ms. Ambrosiano C 301 inf.

198

Mierow, Charles C. "Early Christian Scholar." *Classical Journal* 33 (1937): 3-17.

This is a brief appreciation of the scholarly achievements of St. Jerome.

199

Mullinger, J. Bass. *Schools of Charles the Great and the Restoration of Education in the Ninth Century.* (London, 1877).

200

Murphy, James J. "Saint Augustine and the Age of Transition, A.D. 400 to 1050." In *Rhetoric in the Middle Ages.* Pp. 43-88.

Includes discussions of the encyclopedists, Bede, Boethius, Alcuin, and Rabanus Maurus.

201

Ogilvy, Jack D. A. *Books Known to Anglo-Latin Writers from Aldhelm to Alcuin (670-804).* 2nd ed. (Cambridge, Massachusetts, 1967).

202

Press, Gerald A. "History and the Development of the Idea of History in Antiquity." *History and Theory: Studies in the Philosophy of History* 16 (1977): 280-96.

> *Argues that the idea of "history" was not an important one in antiquity, but that it became so only in Patristic times with rhetorically-trained Christian writers engaged in polemics against pagans.*

203

Quacquarelli, Antonio. *Retorica e liturgia antenicena.* Ricerche patristiche I. (Rome, 1960).

204

Roger, Max. *L'Enseignement des lettres classiques d'Ausone à Alcuin.* (Paris, 1905).

205

Schiudel, U. *Die lateinischen figurenlehren des 5. bis 7. Jahrhunderts und Donats Vergilkommentar (mit zwei Editionen).* Abhandlungen der Akademie der Wissenschaften in Göttingen, philogisch-historische Kasse, folge 91. 3 vols. (Göttingen, 1975).

206

Wallach, Luitpold. "Education and Culture in the Tenth Century." *Medievalia et humanistica* 9 (1955): 18-22.

207

Wildhalm, Gloria-Maria. *Die Rhetorische Elemente in der Regula Benedicti.* Regulae Benedicti Studia, Supplementa. (Hildesheim, 1974).

B. Collection of Texts

208

Halm, Carolus, ed. *Rhetores latini minores.* (Leipzig, 1863). (Reprinted Frankfurt, 1964; Dubuque, Iowa, n.d.)

> *This useful collection of 24 late classical or early medieval Latin texts includes works or fragments by Alcuin, Augustine,*

Bede, and Priscian, as well as the major Ciceronian commentary of Victorinus. It also contains sections on rhetoric from the three major encyclopedists of the transitional period: Isidore of Seville, Cassiodorus, and Martianus Capella.

C. Authors and Works

Alcuin and Pseudo-Alcuin: A. Works

209

Bouhot, Jean Paul, ed. "Alcuin et le 'De catechizandis rudibus' de saint Augustin." *Recherches augustiniennes* 15 (1980): 176-240.

Text of treatise based on Augustine's work of the same name, by an anonymous author (Pseudo-Alcuin) found in an eleventh-century Rouen manuscript.

210

Grammatica. In *PL* 101, cols. 849-902.

211

Howell, Wilbur S., ed. and trans. *Rhetoric of Alcuin and Charlemagne.* (Princeton University Press, 1941).

Howell's introduction traces the Ciceronian and post-classical background of Alcuin's work (written c.792).

Alcuin and Pseudo-Alcuin: B. Secondary References

212

Liénard, Edmond. "Alcuin et les *Epistolae Senecae et Pauli.*" *Revue belge de philologie et d'histoire* 20 (1941): 589-98.

213

Schmitz, Wilhelm. *Alcuins Ars grammatica, die lateinische Schulgrammatik der karolingischen Renaissance.* (Ratingen, 1908).

214
Wallach, Luitpold. *Alcuin and Charlemagne: Studies in Carolingian History and Literature.* (Cornell University Press, 1959).
Wallach devotes part of his study to Alcuin's rhetoric.

215
West, Andrew Fleming. *Alcuin and the Rise of the Christian Schools.* (New York, 1892).

Anselm of Besate: A. Works

216
Bennett, Beth S. "Significance of the *Rhetorimachia* of Anselm of Besate to the History of Rhetoric." *Rhetorica* 5, No. 3 (1987): 231-50.

217
Manitius, Karl, ed. *Rhetorimachia.* In *Gunzo Epistola ad Augienses und Anselm von Besate Rhetorimachia.* MGH, Quellen zur Geistegeschichte des Mittelalters 2. (Weimar, 1958). Pp. 59-183.
Anselm's compendium of rhetorical theory was written between 1046 and 1048.

Augustine of Hippo: A. Works

218
Christopher, Joseph P., ed. and trans. *Augustine's De catechizandis rudibus.* CUAPS 8. (Catholic University of America Press, 1926).
This brief treatise on teaching doctrine to candidates for baptism outlines in rudimentary form Augustine's theory of a new kind of exposition.

219
Dieter, Otto A. L., and William C. Kurth. "*De rhetorica* of Aurelius Augustine." *SM* 35 (1968): 90-108.

220

Leckie, George C., trans. *Concerning the Teacher and on the Immortality of the Soul.* (New York, 1938).

Augustine's short treatise on teaching is useful in understanding his general theory of "sign" which is so important to his rhetorical theory in De doctrina christiana.

221

[Pseudo-Augustine]. *On Rhetoric: Additional Material.* Trans. Joseph M. Miller. In *Readings.* Pp. 6-24.

Translation of De rhetorica quae supersunt *(Halm, pp. 136-151).*

222

Robertson, Durant W., Jr., trans. *On Christian Doctrine.* Library of Liberal Arts 80. (New York, 1958).

Robertson's is the best English translation of Augustine's primary work on the Christian use of rhetoric.

223

Sullivan, Sister Thérèse, trans. *De doctrina christiana liber quartus.* CUAPS 23. (Catholic University of America Press, 1930).

This volume, with good introduction and notes, contains both the Latin text and English translation of the important fourth book of the De Doctrina. *In this book, written in AD 426, about thirty years after books I to III, Augustine states most clearly his support of Cicero's rhetoric.*

224

Vogels, Heinrich J., ed. *De doctrina christiana libros quattuor.* Florilegium patristicum 24. (Bonn, 1930).

This provides a good Latin text of the whole De doctrina christiana.

Augustine of Hippo: B. Bibliography

225
Erickson, Keith V. "Rhetoric and Sermons of Saint Augustine: A Bibliography." *Rhetoric Society Quarterly* 10 (1980): 104-123.

226
Miethe, Terry L. *Augustinian Bibliography, 1970-1980, with Essays on the Fundamentals of Augustinian Scholarship.* (Westport, Connecticut, 1982).

Augustine of Hippo: C. Secondary References

227
Allard, G. H. "L'articulation du sens et du signe dans le *De doctrina christiana* de s. Augustin." *Studia patristica* 14 (1976): 377-88.

228
Brinton, Alan. "St. Augustine and the Problem of Deception in Religious Persuasion." *Religious Studies* 19 (1983): 437-450.

229
Colish, Marcia L. "St. Augustine's Rhetoric of Silence Revisited." *Augustinian Studies* 9 (1978): 15-24.
 See also Mazzeo.

230
Collart, Jean. "Saint Augustin grammarien dans le *De Magistro.*" *Revue des études augustiniennes* 17 (1971): 279-92.

231
Combès, Gustave. *Saint Augustin et la culture classique.* (Paris, 1927).

232
Comeau, Marie. *La Rhétorique de Saint Augustin d'après les tractatus in Ioannem.* (Paris, 1930).

233
Deferrari, R. J. "St. Augustine's Method of Composing and Delivering Sermons." *AJP* 43 (1922): 97-123; 193-219.

234

Erickson, Keith V., ed. *Eloquentia: Saint Augustine on Rhetoric, Signs, and the Sacred Orator.* (Amsterdam, 1985).

A collection of previously-printed essays by a variety of authors.

235

Eskridge, James B. *Influence of Cicero upon Augustine in the Development of his Oratorical Theory for the Training of the Ecclesiastical Orator.* (Menasha, Wisconsin, 1912).

This is a fundamental study of the Isocratean-Ciceronian themes in Augustine's theory of communication. It is important for its rhetorical emphasis, though Eskridge does not fully appreciate Augustine's philosophic background.

236

Finaert, Joseph. *Saint Augustin rhéteur.* (Paris, 1939).

237

Fortin, Ernest L. "Augustine and the Problem of Christian Rhetoric." *Augustinian Studies* 5 (1974): 85-100.

238

Francey, Thérèse. *Les idées litteraires de Saint Augustin dans le* De doctrina christiana. (Stockholm, 1923).

Includes a section covering Augustine's indebtedness to Cicero and Quintilian in the DDC.

239

Hill, E. "*De doctrina christiana*: A Suggestion." *Studia patristica* 6 (1959): 443-46.

240

Hogger, Joseph. *Die Kinderpsychologie Augustins.* Beiträge zur Erziehungswissenschaft 4. (Munich, 1937).

241

Howie, George. *Educational Theory and Practice in St. Augustine.* (Columbia University Press, 1969).

242
Huppé, Bernard F. *Doctrine and Poetry: Augustine's Influence on Old English Poetry.* (State University of New York Press, 1959).

243
Jackson, Darrell B. "Theory of Signs in Saint Augustine's *De doctrina christiana.*" In *Augustine: A Collection Critical Essays.* Ed. R.A. Markus. (Garden City, New York, 1972). Pp. 92-147.

244
Jansen, François. "Saint Augustin et la rhétorique." *Nouvelle revue théologique* 57 (1930): 282-97.

245
Jiménez, Jesus G. "La Retórica de San Agustín y su patrimonio clásico." *La Ciudad de Dios* 6 (1955): 11-32.

246
Johnson, W.R. "Isocrates Flowering: The Rhetoric of Augustine." *Philsophy and Rhetoric* 9 (1976): 217-231.

247
Jubany, Narciso. "San Agustín y la formación oratoria cristiana: estudio comparado del libro IV 'De doctrina christiana' y del 'De catechizandis rudibus.'" *Analecta sacra Tarraconensia* 15 (1942): 9-22.

248
Kevane, Eugene. "Augustine's *De doctrina christiana*: A Treatise on Christian Education." *Recherches augustiniennes* 4 (1966): 97-133.
    For an opposing view see Verheijen.

249
Kevane, Eugene. "*Translatio imperii*: Augustine's *De doctrina christiana* and the Classical *Paideia.*" *Studia Patristica* 14 (1976): 446-60.

250
Markus, R.A. "Saint Augustine on Signs." In *Augustine: A Collection of Critical Essays.* Ed. R.A. Markus. (Garden City, New York, 1972). Pp. 61-91.

251

Marrou, Henri. *Saint Augustin et la fin de la culture antique.* Bibliothèque des écoles françaises d'Athènes et de Rome 145. (Paris, 1938).

252

Marrou, Henri. *Saint Augustine and His Influence through the Ages.* Trans. Patrick Hepburne-Scott. (New York, 1957).

This attractive volume makes an excellent introduction to the breadth of Augustine's interests and his influence.

253

Mazzeo, Joseph. "St. Augustine's Rhetoric of Silence." *Journal of the History of Ideas* 23 (1962): 175-196.

See also Colish.

254

Murphy, James J. "Saint Augustine and the Debate about a Christian Rhetoric." *QJS* 46 (1960): 400-10.

This article summarizes the conflicting views in the fourth-century church concerning the value of pagan learning, and describes Augustine's decisive support in retaining rhetoric for use by preachers and apologists. Published in revised form as part of chapter two in Murphy, Rhetoric in the Middle Ages.

255

Oroz, José. "El 'De doctrina christiana' o la retórica cristiana." *Estudios clásicos* 3 (1956): 452-9.

256

Parsons, Sister Wilfrid. *Study of the Vocabulary and Rhetoric of the Letters of Saint Augustine.* CUAPS 3. (Catholic University of America Press, 1923).

257

Pépin, Jean. "Saint Augustin et la fonction protreptique de l'allégorie." *Recherches augustiniennes* I (1958): 243-86.

258

Press, Gerald A. "Content and Argument of Augustine's 'De doctrina christiana.'" *Augustiniana* 31 (1981): 165-82.

Includes a detailed outline of the book to demonstrate its unity. Praises the book as a tractatio scripturarum, *capable of serving several purposes simultaneously.*

259

Press, Gerald A. "*Doctrina* in Augustine's *De doctrina christiana.*" *Philosophy and Rhetoric* 17 (1984): 98-120.

This well-documented study argues that the meaning of doctrina *in the title is complex, and that Augustine deliberately uses its variety of meanings to construct a new ideal for Christian culture.*

260

Press, Gerald A. "Subject and Structure of Augustine's *De doctrina christiana.*" *Augustinian Studies* 11 (1980): 99-124.

One of the most useful recent studies, since the author surveys a variety of modern interpretations, analyzes Augustine's use of the rhetorical tradition, and finally offers his own view that the book transforms classical rhetorical theory to meet the needs of the new Christian culture.

261

Semple, W. H. "Augustinus Rhetor: A Study, from the *Confessions,* of St. Augustine's secular career in education." *JEH* I (1950): 135-50.

262

Testard, Maurice. *Saint Augustine et Cicéron.* Etudes augustiniennes. 2 vols. (Paris, 1958).

Despite its intriguing title this is a rather poorly arranged volume largely concerned with tracing sources of individual quotations. Eskridge is far more useful.

263

Vance, Eugène. "Saint Augustine: Language as Temporality." In *Mimesis: From Mirror to Method, Augustine to Descartes.* Ed. John D. Lyons and Stephen G. Nichols Jr. (Hanover, New Hampshire, 1982). Pp. 279-92.

264

Verheijen, L. M. J. "Le *De doctrina christiana* de saint Augustin." *Augustiniana* 24 (1974): 10-20.

Bede: A. Works

265

De arte metrica. In *Grammatici latini 7.* Ed. Heinrich Keil. (Leipzig, 1880). Pp. 227-60.

266

De schematibus et tropis. In *Rhetores latini minores.* Ed. Carolus Halm. (Leipzig, 1863). Pp. 607-18. (Reprinted Frankfurt, 1964; Dubuque, Iowa, n.d.)

This brief treatise, apparently the first grammatical work written by an Englishman, is based on the Barbarismus *of the Roman grammarian Donatus but cites 122 scriptural examples of tropes and figures instead of the classical examples given by Donatus.*

267

Kendall, Calvin B., ed. *De arte metrica. De schematibus et tropis.* In *Bedae venerabilis Opera VI: Opera didascalica 1.* Ed. Charles W. Jones. (Turnhout, 1975).

Includes the commentary of Remigius Auxerre, edited by Margot H. King. Jones's Introduction to the volume provides a fine survey of early medieval educational practices.

268

Tanenhaus, Gussie Hecht. "Bede's *De schematibus et tropis*: A Translation." *QJS* 48 (1962): 237-53.

Reprinted in Readings in Medieval Rhetoric *(pp.97-122).*

Bede: B. Secondary References

269

Bolton, W. F. "Bede Bibliography, 1935-1960." *Traditio* 18 (1962): 436-45.

270

Isola, Antonio. "Il 'De schematibus et tropis' di Beda in rapporto al 'De doctrina christiana' di Agostino." *Romano Barbarica* (Rome) 1 (1976): 71-82.

271
King, Margot H. *"Grammatica mystica*: A Study of Bede's Grammatical Curriculum." In *Saints, Scholars and Heroes: Studies in Medieval Culture in Honour of Charles W. Jones.* Ed. Margot H. King and Wesley M. Stevens. Vol. 1 of 2. (Collegeville, Minnesota, 1979). Pp. 145-59.

Boethius: A. Works

272
Boethius's De topicis differentiis. Trans. Eleonore Stump. (Cornell University Press, 1978).

273
Boethius's In Ciceronis Topica. Trans. Eleonore Stump. (Cornell University Press, 1988).
> *This lucid translation is accompanied by good explanatory notes. Stump includes an Appendix (pp. 244-255) on Categories and Predicables "to make the reader acquainted with the technical ancient and scholastic notions of the categories, predicables, and the Porphyrian Tree, which pervade scholastic philosophy."*

274
De differentiis topicis libri quatuor. In *PL* 64, cols. 1173-216.

275
Elenchorum sophisticorum Aristotelis libri duo. In *PL* 64, cols. 1007-40.

276
In topica Ciceronis commentariorum libri sex. In *PL* 64, cols. 1039-174.

277
Liber de definitione. In *PL* 64, cols. 891-910.

278
Locorum rhetoricorum distinctio. In *PL* 64, cols. 1221-4.

279

Overview of the Structure of Rhetoric. Trans. Joseph M. Miller. In *Readings.* Pp. 70-76.

Translation of Speculatio de cognatione rhetoricae Boethii.

280

[Pseudo-Boethius]. *De disciplina scholarium.* In *PL* 64, cols. 1223-38.

This students' manual, long attributed to Boethius, was actually composed c. A.D. 1230-40. It includes encouragement of oral expression in preparation for university work.

281

Speculatio de rhetoricae cognatione. In *PL* 64, cols. 1217-22.

282

Topicorum Aristotelis libri octo. In *PL* 64, cols. 909-1008.

These items reveal Boethius' concern for rhetoric; however, he discusses only Cicero in this connection, not apparently having access to Aristotle's Rhetoric.

Boethius: B. Secondary References

283

Alfonsi, Luigi. "Studii Boeziani." *Aevum* 19 (1945): 142-57.

284

Courcelle, Pierre. "Boèce et l'école d'Alexandrie." *Mélanges d'archéologie et d'histoire* 52 (1935): 185-223.

285

Gibson, Margaret T., ed. *Boethius: His Life, Thought and Influence.* (Oxford, 1981).

Although the seventeen essays in this volume include two studies of Boethius' logic and three of the quadrivium, *there are only scattered references to his* In Ciceronis topicis *and other works with rhetorical implications.*

286

Leff, Michael C. "Boethius and the History of Medieval Rhetoric." *Central States Speech Journal* 25 (1974): 135-141.

> *Concludes that rising use of Boethius' De differentiis topicis, Book IV, in the high middle ages was matched by a decline of interest in holistic classical rhetoric.*

287
Leff, Michael C. "Logician's Rhetoric: Boethius' *De differentiis topicis, Book IV." In Medieval Eloquence.* Pp. 3-24.

288
Leff, Michael C. "Topics of Argumentative Invention in Latin Rhetorical Theory from Cicero to Boethius." *Rhetorica* 1 (1983): 23-44.

> *This perceptive analysis of "the persistent tension between form and matter in topical invention" includes an appendix outlining the doctrine of Attributes of the Person and the Act in Cicero, Fortunatianus, Julius Victor, and Martianus Capella.*

289
Lerer, Seth. *Boethius and Dialogue.* (Princeton University Press, 1985).

290
Obertello, Luca. *Severino Boezio.* Academia Ligure di Scienze e Lettere, Collana di Monografie. 2 vols. (Genoa, 1974).

> *The second volume is a bibliography (pp. 7-308) of works by and about Boethius.*

291
Solmsen, Friedrich. "Boethius and the History of the *Organon.*" *AJP* 65 (1944): 69-74.

Cassiodorus: A. Works

292
In psalterium expositio. In *PL* 70, cols. 25-1056.

> *An analysis of the tropes and figures used in the Scriptural text.*

293

Jones, Leslie Webber, trans. *Introduction to Divine and Human Readings*. (Columbia University Press, 1946).

This translation of Cassiodorus' sixth-century encyclopedic work is accompanied by a useful introduction. Compare Isidore and Martianus Capella.

294

Mynors, Roger A. B., ed. *Cassiodori senatoris institutiones divinarumet saecularium litterarum*. (Oxford, 1963).

The Latin text of the encyclopedic work translated by Jones (above).

Cassiodorus: B. Secondary References

295

Halporn, James W. "Manuscripts of Cassiodorus' 'Expositio Psalmorum.'" *Traditio* 37 (1981): 388-96.

Lists 120 manuscripts of this popular treatment of the Psalms which includes notations on the rhetorical figures used.

296

Lagorio, Valerie M. "Text of Cassiodorus's *De rhetorica* in Codex Pal. Lat. 1588." *Scriptorium* 30 (1976): 43-45.

297

O'Donnell, James J. *Cassiodorus*. (University of California Press, 1979).

A definitive study of his career and works, including the Variae *(letter collection), the* Expositio Psalmorum *(stylistic analysis of some later influence), and* Institutiones *(his major encyclopedia).*

Donatus

298

Holtz, Louis. *Donat et la tradition de l'enseignement grammatical: Étude sur l'"Ars Donati" et sa diffusion (IVᵉ-IXᵉ siècles) et édition critique*. Documents, études et répertoires. Publiés par l'Institut de Recherche et d'Histoire des Textes. (Paris, 1981).

This massive (782 page) study is indispensable to an understanding of the Donatic tradition.

Isidore of Seville: A. Works

299

Cerino, Dorothy V. "Rhetoric and Dialectic of Isidorus of Seville: A Translation and Commentary." Unpublished MA thesis, Brooklyn College, 1938.

300

Etymologies, II. 1-15: 'Concerning Rhetoric.' Trans. Dorothy V. Cerino. In *Readings*. Pp. 79-95.

The translation is from the 1938 M.A. Thesis of Cerino.

301

Lindsay, Wallace M., ed. *Etymologiarum sive originum libri XX*. 2 vols. (Oxford, 1911). (Reprinted Oxford, 1985.)

This famous seventh-century encyclopedic work begins with three books on grammar, rhetoric, and dialectic. Compare Cassiodorus and Martianus Capella.

Isidore of Seville: B. Secondary References

302

Brehaut, Ernest. *Encyclopedist of the Dark Ages: Isidore of Seville*. (Columbia University Press, 1912).

303

Fontaine, Jacques. *Isidore de Séville et la culture classique dans l'Espagne wisigothique*. (Paris, 1959).

304

Fontaine, Jacques. "Théorie et pratique du style chez Isidore de Séville." *Vigiliae christianae* 14 (1960): 65-101.

Julian of Toledo: A. Works

305

Lindsay, Wallace M., ed. *De vitiis et figuris.* St. Andrew's University Publications 15. (Oxford University Press, 1922).

306

Maestre Yenes, Maria A.H., ed. *Ars Iuliani Toletani episcopi. Una gramática latina de la España visigoda. Estudio y edición critica.* Publicaciones del Instituto Provincial de Investigaciones y Estudios Toledanos, serie segunda: "Vestigios del pasado," 5. (Toledo, 1973).

Julian of Toledo: B. Secondary References

307

Beeson, Charles H. "Ars Grammatica of Julian of Toledo." *Miscellanea Francesco Ehrle I.* (Rome, 1924).

308

Bischoff, Bernhard. "Ein Brief Julians von Toledo über Rhythmen, metrische Dichtung und Prosa." *Hermes* 87 (1959): 247-56.

Martianus Capella: A. Works

309

Dick, [Wilhelm] Adolfus, ed. *De nuptiis philologiae et mercurii.* In *Martianus Capella.* (Leipzig, 1925).

> *The flowery preface to the section on* rhetorica *in this encyclopedic work was often repeated during the middle ages, though the routine compendium of rhetorical lore following the introduction was usually ignored. Compare Cassiodorus and Isidore.*

310
Stahl, William Harris and Richard Johnson, with E.L. Burge, trans. *The Marriage of Philology and Mercury*. Vol. 2 of *Martianus Capella and the Seven Liberal Arts*. 2 vols. (Columbia University Press, 1977).

Martianus Capella: B. Secondary References

311
Fischer, Hans. *Untersuchung über die Quellen der Rhetorik des Martianus Capella*. (Breslau, 1936).

Miscellaneous Authors

312
Fichtenau, Heinrich. "Rhetorische Elemente in der ottonisch-salischen Herrscherurkunde." *MIÖG* 68 (1960): 39-62.

Notker Labeo: A. Works

313
Piper, Paul, ed. *De arte rhetorica* (partly lost). In *Die Schriften Notkers und seiner Schule*. Germanischer Bücherschatz 8-10. 3 vols. (Freiburg and Tübingen, 1882-3).

Notker Labeo: B. Secondary References

314
Dieter, Otto A. L. "Rhetoric of Notker Labeo." In *Papers in Rhetoric*. Ed. Donald C. Bryant. (St. Louis, 1940). Pp. 27-33.
The little volume in which this appears was privately printed and therefore difficult to obtain.

315
Jaffe, Samuel. "Antiquity and Innovation in Notker's *Nova rhetorica* : The Doctrine of Invention." *Rhetorica* 3 (1985): 165-81.

316

Sonderegger, Stefan. "Notker der Deutsche und Cicero: Aspekte einer mittelalterlichen Rezeption." In *Florilegium Sangallense. Festschrift für Johannes Duft zum 65. Geburtstag.* Ed. O.P. Clavadetscher et al. (Saint Gall, 1980). Pp. 243-266.

Onulf of Speyer: A. Works

317

Wattenbach, Wilhelm, ed. "Magister Onulf von Speier." *Sitzungs der königlich preussischen Akademie der Wissenschaften zu Berlin* 20 (1894): 361-86.

>This is an edition of the Colores rhetorici with an introduction.

Onulf of Speyer: B. Secondary References

318

Wallach, Luitpold. "Onulf of Speyer: A Humanist of the Eleventh Century." *Medievalia et Humanistica* 6 (1950): 35-56.

Origen

319

Daniélou, Jean. *Origen.* Trans. Walter Mitchell. (New York, 1955).

>This study is especially important for an understanding of the influence in the West of the Alexandrian practice of non-literal interpretation of texts, particularly in preaching.

320

Jennings, Margaret. "Art of the Pseudo-Origen Homily 'De Maria Magdalena.'" *Medievalia et Humanistica* 5 (1974): 139-52.

Priscian: A. Works

321

Fundamentals Adapted from Hermogenes. Trans. Joseph M. Miller. In *Readings.* Pp. 52-68.

> *Translation of* Praeexercitamina Prisciani Grammatici ex Hermogene versa *(Halm, 551-560).*

322

Hertz, Martin, ed. *Institutionum grammaticarum.* In *Grammatici latini.* Ed. Heinrich Keil. 7 vols. (Leipzig, 1853-1880). Vol. 2 (Leipzig, 1855), 1-597 and Vol. 3 (Leipzig, 1859), 1-384.

> *Priscian's sixth-century Latin grammar, more advanced than the simple primers of Donatus, became a staple text for almost a thousand years.*

323

Keil, Heinrich, ed. *Praeexercitamina.* Vol. 3 of *Grammatici latini.* (Leipzig, 1959). Pp. 430-40 (Also in *Rhetores latini minores,* ed. Carolus Halm [Leipzig, 1863], 551-60). (Reprinted Hildesheim, 1981.)

> *This is a collection of elementary composition exercises* (progymnasmata). *While not widely circulated during the middle ages, it appeared from time to time in various parts of Europe.*

Priscian: B. Secondary References

324

Clark, Donald L. "Rhetoric and the Literature of the English Middle Ages." *QJS* 45 (1959): 19-28.

> *Despite its title, this deals with the medieval influence of Priscian.*

Rabanus Maurus: A. Works

325

Knöpfler, Aloisius, ed. *De institutione clericorum.* Veröffentlichungen aus dem Kirchenhistorischen Seminar München 5. (Munich, 1900). (Also *PL* 107, cols. 293-420). *Rabanus includes directions to preachers, relying heavily on Augustine's* De doctrina christiana.

Rabanus Maurus: B. Secondary References

326

Blumenkranz, B. "Raban Maur et Saint Augustine: compilation ou adaptation? A propos du latin biblique." *Revue du moyen âge latin* 7 (1951): 97-110.

327

Böhue, W., ed. *Hrabanus Maurus und seine Schule. Festschrift der Rabanus-Maurus-Schule.* Fuldaer Geschichtsblätter 56, 1980. (Fulda, 1980).

Remigius of Auxerre: A. Works

328

Fox, W., ed. *In artem Donati minorem commentum ad fidem codicum manuscriptorum.* (Leipzig, 1902).

329

Lutz, Cora E., ed. *Commentum in Martianum Capellam.* 2 vols. (Leiden, 1962 and 1965).

Remigius of Auxerre: B. Secondary References

330

Elder, J. P. "Did Remigius of Auxerre Comment on Bede's *De schematibus et tropis?*" *MS* 9 (1947): 141-50.

331
Lutz, Cora E. "Commentary of Remigius of Auxerre on Martianus Capella." *MS* 19 (1957): 137-56.

332
Lutz, Cora E. "Remigius' Ideas on the Classification of the Seven Liberal Arts." *Traditio* 12 (1956): 65-86.

Victorinus

333
Q. Fabii Laurentii Victorini Explanationum in Rhetoricam M. Tullii Ciceronis libri duo. Ed. Charles Halm. In *Rhetores latini minores.* (Leipzig, 1863). Pp. 155-304. (Reprinted Frankfurt, 1964; Dubuque, Iowa, n.d.)

This late classical commentary on Cicero's De inventione *was widely distributed during the middle ages, surviving in 50 manuscripts according to Ward.*

III
High Middle Ages

The main works of the ancient world had varying fates in the middle ages. Cicero was the acknowledged "Master of Eloquence" for the period, his fame resting mainly on his youthful *De inventione* and on the anonymous *Rhetorica ad Herennium* universally attributed to him. His mature *De oratore* was little known. Commentaries on Roman rhetorical treatises in this period are therefore an important index to the influence of Cicero. Aristotle on the other hand was influential primarily through two dialectical works that laid the groundwork for the medieval disputation; his *Rhetoric* was largely ignored by theorists studying communication. Quintilian's *Institutio oratoria*, in a shortened version, had a short-lived revival in the twelfth century, then virtually disappeared until Poggio Bracciolini rediscovered a complete text at St. Gall in 1416—an event essentially marking the end of the medieval phase of rhetorical history. The sophistic works of men like Aphthonius and Hermogenes play no part in this period; they became important again only in the fifteenth-century Renaissance.

The medieval history of the grammatical tradition is so complex that a separate section is set aside for it in chapter 5 with the "Arts of Poetry" taught by the grammar masters.

A. General Studies

334
Benson, R.L., Giles Constable, Carol D. Lanham, eds. *Renaissance and Renewal in the Twelfth Century*. Papers from a conference held under the auspices of the UCLA Center for Medieval and Renaissance Studies and the Harvard University Committee on Medieval Studies, 26 -29 November, 1977, commemorating the contribution by Charles Homer Haskins. (Oxford, 1982).
Some 26 articles.

335
Bliese, John. "Study of Rhetoric in the Twelfth Century." *QJS* 63 (1977): 364-383.
A survey of secondary sources concerning the teaching of rhetoric "as a liberal art," eleventh through thirteenth centuries.

336
Evans, Gillian R. "Place of Peter the Chanter's *De Tropis Loquendi*." *Analecta Cisterciensia* 39 (1983): 231-253.
Peter's De Tropis Loquendi *deals with theological language in light of grammar, rhetoric, and logic.*

337
Evans, Gillian R. "'Studium discendi': Otloh of St. Emmeram and the Seven Liberal Arts." *Recherches de Théologie ancienne et médiévale* 44 (1977): 29-54.

338
Gualazzini, Ugo. *Trivium e quadrivium*. Iùs Romanum Medii Aevi, Pars I.5a. (Milan, 1974).
Includes a section on "la retorica e le discipline giuridiche" (in

chapter three) and devotes the fifth chapter to "Il dritto e la crisi della retorica."

339

Haskins, Charles H. "List of Text-books from the Close of the Twelfth Century." *Harvard Studies in Classical Philology* 20 (1909): 75-94.

This frequently quoted source is narrow in scope.

340

Huygens, R.B.C., ed. *Accessus ad auctores.* Collection Latomus 15. (Brussels, 1954).

341

Jacob, Ernst F. "Some Aspects of Classical Influence in Mediaeval England." In *Vorträge der Bibliothek Warburg, 1930-1931.* (Leipzig, 1932). Pp. 1-27.

342

Kennan, Elizabeth T. "Rhetoric and Style in the 'De Consideratione' [of Bernard of Clairvaux]." In *Studies in Medieval Cistercian History II.* Ed. John R. Sommerfeldt. (Kalamazoo, Michigan, 1976). Pp. 40-48.

343

Maccagnolo, E. *Thierry of Chartres, Guglielmo di Conches, Bernardo Silvestre: Il Divino e il Megacosmo. Testi Filosofici e Scientifici della Scuola di Chartres.* (Milan, 1980).

344

McInerny, Ralph. "Beyond the Liberal Arts." In *The Seven Liberal Arts in the Middle Ages.* Ed. David L. Wagner. (Indiana University Press, 1983). Pp. 248-272.

Appraises (and refutes) several common misconceptions about the actual teaching of the seven liberal arts during the middle ages.

345

Murphy, James J. "Rhetoric in Fourteenth-Century Oxford." *MAE* 34 (1965): 1-20.

This article includes a survey of the medieval history of the four ancient traditions of discourse: Aristotelian, Ciceronian, grammatical, and Sophistic, together with a description of rhetoric in late fourteenth-century Oxford. For a critique of the argument see Schoeck.

346
O'Donnell, J. Reginald. "*Rhetorica divina* of William of Auvergne: A Study in Applied Rhetoric." In *Images of Man in Ancient and Medieval Thought. Studia Gerardo Verbeke ab amicis et collegis dicata.* Ed. F. Bossier et al. (Louvain, 1976). Pp. 323-333.
Discusses William's use of rhetoric in a treatise on prayer (written c. 1240) also known as Ars oratoria eloquentiae divinae.

347
Paulmier-Foucart, M. "L'Atelier Vincent de Beauvais. Recherches sur l'état des connaissances au Moyen Âge d'après une encyclopédie du XIIIe siècle." *Le Moyen Age* 85 (1979): 87-99.

348
Scaglione, Aldo. "Aspetti delle arti del trivio fra medioevo e rinascimento." *Medioevo Romanzo* 3 (1976): 265-291.

349
Schoeck, Richard. "On Rhetoric in Fourteenth Century Oxford." *Mediaeval Studies* 30 (1968): 214-55.

350
Steel, Carlos G. "Etica e retorica: Considerazioni su un problema attuale partendo dal pensiero antico e medievale." *Tijdschrift voor Theologie* 41 (1979): 405-32.

351
Stock, Brian. *The Implications of Literacy: Written Language and Models of Interpretation in the Eleventh and Twelfth Centuries.* (Princeton University Press, 1983).

352
Wagner, David L. "Seven Liberal Arts and Classical Scholarship." In *The Seven Liberal Arts in the Middle Ages.* Ed. David L. Wagner. (Indiana University Press, 1983). Pp. 1-31.
Sketches the development of the concept of "liberal arts."

B. Aristotle

I. Works and Commentaries

353

Butterworth, Charles E., ed. and trans. *Averroës' Three Short Commentaries on Aristotle's 'Topics,' 'Rhetoric,' and 'Poetics'.* (State University of New York Press, 1977).

> *Averroës (1126-1198) was one of the best known Arabic commentators on Aristotle—sometimes referred to simply as "The Commentator"—and Butterworth's valuable comments in this volume explain his theories well.*

354

De arte poetica Guillelmo de Moerbeke interprete. Ed. Valgimigli, Erse. Revised preface and indices by Ezio Franceschini and L. Minio-Paluello. Aristoteles Latinus 33. (Bruges, 1953).

> *Aristotle's* Poetics *was little used in the middle ages.*

355

Schneider, Bernd. *Aristoteles. Rhetorica. Translatio anonyma sive Vetus et translatio Guillelmi de Moerbeka.* Aristoteles latinus, XXXI, 1-2. (Leiden, 1978).

> *Texts of two of the three major medieval Latin translations of the* Rhetorica *(the third being that of Hermannus Allemanus). The Moerbeke version, completed at Paris about 1269 under the aegis of the Aquinas circle, had the greatest circulation and survives in nearly 100 manuscripts.*

356

Spengel, Leonard, ed. *Aristotelis ars rhetorica: accedit vetusta translatio latina.* 2 vols. (Leipzig, 1867).

> *In vol. 1, 178-342 is the text of the Latin translation by William of Moerbeke. The incipit is* Rhetorica assecutiva dialecticae est.

II. Pseudo-Aristotle: *Rhetorica ad Alexandrum*

357
Dittmeyer, Leonhard. "Die lateinische Übersetzung der pseudo-aristotelischen Rhetorica ad Alexandrum aus dem 13. Jahrhundert." *Bayerische Blätter für das Gymnasial-schulwesen* 69 (1933): 157-65.

358
Dittmeyer, Leonhard. "Hat Bartholomaeus von Messina die Rhetorica ad Alexandrum übersetzt?" *Philologische Wochenschrift* 58 (1938): 252-6, 286-8.

359
Dittmeyer, Leonhard. "Neue Beiträge zur lateinischen Übersetzung der pseudo-aristotelischen Rhetorica ad Alexandrum aus dem 13. Jahrhundert." *Bayerische Blätter für das Gymnasial-schulwesen* 70 (1934): 166-72.

360
Fuhrmann, Manfred, ed. *Anaximenes Lampsacus ars rhetorica.* (Leipzig, 1966).

361
Grabmann, Martin. "Eine lateinische Übersetzung der pseudo-aristotelischen Rhetorica ad Alexandrum aus dem 13. Jahrhundert." SBAW, Heft 4, 1931-2. (Munich, 1932).
At least three medieval Latin translations were made of this rhetorical compendium probably composed shortly after Aristotle's death.

III. Giles of Rome [Aegidius Romanus]: A. Works

362
Achillinus, Alexander, ed. *Commentaria in rhetoricam Aristotelis.* (Venice, 1515). (Reprinted Frankfurt, 1968.)
This work is the complete text of the Moerbeke translation of the Rhetorica with a lengthy seriatim commentary of about 1280 by Giles of Rome; this is the only surviving medieval Latin commentary on the complete Rhetorica. *Giles of Rome*

(Aegidius Romanus) is also known as Egidio Colonna. On pages 2ᵛ5ʳ appears a treatise, of obscure origin and date, that purports to discuss the Rhetorica *in light of the* De scientiis *of the ninth-century Arab writer, al-Farabi. This treatise is generally called the* Alpharabi epithoma *or referred to by its incipit,* Declaratio compendiosa per viam diuisionis Alpharab[ii] super libros rhetoricorum Aristotelis.

363

Bruni, Gerardo. "'De differentia rhetoricae, ethicae et politicae' of Aegidius Romanus." *New Scholasticism* 6 (1932): 1-18.

The article includes the text of the very short piece by Giles of Rome on the relations between the three subjects named. Its comments on Cicero indicate that it was apparently written after Giles' full commentary on Aristotle's Rhetoric.

364

On the Difference between Rhetoric, Ethics, and Politics Part I. Trans. Joseph M. Miller. In *Readings.* Pp. 265-268.

Translation of opening section of De differentia rhetoricae, ethicae et politicae *from the text of Bruni.*

III. Giles of Rome [Aegidius Romanus]: B. Secondary References

365

Murphy, James J. "Scholastic Condemnation of Rhetoric in the Commentary of Giles of Rome on the *Rhetoric* of Aristotle." In *Arts libéraux et philosophie au moyen âge.* Actes du quatrième congrès international de philosophie médiévale. (Montreal, 1969). Pp. 833-41.

366

O'Donnell, J. Reginald. "Commentary of Giles of Rome on the *Rhetoric* of Aristotle." In *Essays in Medieval History Presented to Bertie Wilkinson.* Ed. Thayron A. Sandquist and Michael R. Powicke. (University of Toronto Press, 1969).

367
Robert, Brother S., F.S.C. "Rhetoric and Dialectic: According to the First Latin Commentary on the *Rhetoric* of Aristotle." *New Scholasticism* 31 (1957): 484-498.

IV. Aristotle: Secondary References

368
Arens, Hans. *Aristotle's Theory of Language and Its Tradition: Texts from 500 to 1750.* Studies in the History of Linguistics, 29. (Amsterdam, 1984).

369
Boggess, William F. "Hermannus Alemannus's Rhetorical Translations." *Viator* 2 (1971): 227-50.

370
Bottin, L. *Contributi della tradizione greco-latina e arabo-latina al testo della "Retorica" di Aristotele.* Studia Aristotelica, 8. (Padua, 1977).

371
Callus, Daniel. "Introduction of Aristotelian Learning to Oxford." *PBA* 29 (1943): 229-81.

372
Cranz, F.E. "Editions of the Latin Aristotle Accompanied by the Commentaries of Averroës." In *Philosophy and Humanism: Renaissance Essays in Honor of P.O. Kristeller.* Ed. Edward P. Mahoney. (Columbia University Press, 1976). Pp. 116-128.

373
Ferreiro Alemparte, J. "Hermann el alemán, Traductor del siglo XIII en Toledo." *Hispania Sacra* 35 (1983): 9-48.
   Includes a discussion of Hermannus Allemanus' translation of Aristotle's Rhetoric.

374
Franceschini, Ezio. "La 'Poetica' di Aristotele nel secolo XIII." *Atti del reale istituto Veneto di scienze, lettere ed arti* 94, part 2 (1934-5): 523-48.

375

Fredborg, Karin Margareta. "Buridan's *Quaestiones super Rhetoricam Aristotelis.*" In *The Logic of John Buridan: Acts of the 3rd European Symposium on Medieval Logic and Semantics, Copenhagen 16-21 November, 1975.* Ed. Jan Pinborg. (Copenhagen, 1976). Pp. 47-59.

> *Discussion of 127* Quaestiones *(edited p. 55-59) surviving in three manuscripts. Argues that existence of* quaestiones *is proof of rhetoric's role in the university. Concludes that Buridan's questions attempt to sharpen the definition of limits for the scope of rhetoric.*

376

Grabmann, Martin. "Aristoteles im zwoelften Jahrhundert." *MS* 12 (1950): 123-62.

377

Grabmann, Martin. *Forschungen über die lateinischen Aristoteles-übersetzungen des XIII. Jahrhunderts.* Beiträge zur Geschichte der Philosophie des Mittelalters 17, Heft 5-6. (Münster, 1916).

378

Grabmann, Martin. *Methoden und Hilfsmittel des Aristoteles-studiums im Mittelalter.* SBAW, Heft 5, 1939. (Munich, 1939).

379

Hultzén, Lee S. "Aristotle's *Rhetoric* in England to 1600." unpublished PH D thesis, Cornell University, 1932.

380

Jourdain, Amable. *Recherches critiques sur l'âge et l'origine des traductions latines d'Aristote et sur des commentaires grecs ou arabes employés par les docteurs scolastiques.* (Paris, 1843). (Reprinted New York, 1960.)

381

Kelly, Henry Ansgar. "Aristotle-Averroes-Allemannus on Tragedy: The Influence of the 'Poetics' [of Aristotle] on the Latin Middle Ages." *Viator* 10 (1979): 161-209.

> *Argues that the* Poetics *had little influence even though there are a number of citations of it by a number of authors.*

382
Lacombe, G., A. Birkenmajer, M. Dulong, and Ezio Franceschini, eds. *Aristoteles latinus: codices.* Supplements and indices by L. Minio-Paluello, 2 vols., Corpus Philosophorum Medii Aevi, part II. (Vol. 1, Rome, 1939; Vol. 2, Cambridge, England, 1955).
This is an indispensable bibliographic guide for students of the medieval history of Aristotle's works, and includes manuscript inventories for each work.

383
Lacombe, G., A. Birkenmajer, M. Dulong, and Ezio Franceschini, eds. *Aristoteles latinus: codices.* Supplements and indices by L. Minio-Paluello, 2 vols., Corpus Philosophorum Medii Aevi, part I. (Bruges and Paris, 1957).

384
Lacombe, G., A. Birkenmajer, M. Dulong, and Ezio Franceschini, eds. *Aristoteles latinus: codices. Supplementa altera,* ed. L. Minio-Paluello. (Bruges and Paris, 1961).

385
Murphy, James J. "Aristotle's *Rhetoric* in the Middle Ages." *QJS* 52 (1966): 109-15.
This article discusses the comparative neglect of Aristotle's Rhetoric *in the middle ages. It includes a table of manuscript groupings indicating that medieval bookmakers tended to bind the* Rhetoric *with ethical and moral works rather than with dialectical or rhetorical works.*

386
Murphy, James J. "Earliest Teaching of Rhetoric at Oxford." *SM* 27 (1960): 345-7.
Murphy argues that Aristotle's Rhetoric *did not figure in Oxford teaching prior to 1431.*

387
Schneider, Bernd. *Die mittelalterlichen Griechisch-Lateinischen Übersetzungen der Aristotelischen Rhetorik.* Peripatoi: Philologisch-Historische Studien zum Aristotelismus, 2. (Berlin, 1971).

Discusses three major Greek-to-Latin translations: Translatio vetus, Translatio Guillelmi, *and* Translatio antiqui.

388

Van Steenberghen, Fernand. *Aristotle in the West.* Trans. Leonard Johnston. (Louvain, 1955).

This volume includes a useful summary of the work of Arabic writers (al-Farabi, Averroës, etc.) on Aristotle.

389

Wartelle, André. *Inventaire des manuscrits grecs d'Aristote et de ses commentateurs.* (Paris, 1963).

C. Cicero and Pseudo-Cicero

I. General Cicero Studies

390

Baron, Hans. "Cicero and the Roman Civic Spirit in the Middle Ages and Early Renaissance." *Bulletin of the John Rylands Library* 22 (1938): 72-97.

391

Evans, Gillian R. "Two Aspects of 'Memoria' in Eleventh and Twelfth Century Writings." *Classica et Medievalia* 32 (1971-80): 263-78.

Compares two traditions, one stemming from the Rhetorica ad Herennium *and the other from more general studies. Includes a discussion of memory in John of Salisbury, Hugh of St. Victor, and Alain de Lille.*

392

Finch, C.E. "Text of Cicero's 'Topica' in Codex Chartres 498." *Mediaeval Studies* 40 (1978): 468-72.

393

Fredborg, Karin Margareta. "Twelfth-Century Ciceronian Rhetoric: Its Doctrinal Development and Influences." In *Rhetoric*

Revalued: Papers from the International Society for the History of Rhetoric. Ed. Brian Vickers. (Binghamton, New York, 1982). Pp. 87-97.

394

Quadlbauer, Franz. "Zur Nachwirkung und Wandlung des ciceronischen Rednerideals." In *Ars rhetorica: antica et nuova.* Publicazioni dell'Istituto di filologia classica e medievale dell'Università di Genova, 83. (Genoa, 1983). Pp. 77-116.

395

Rand, Edward K. *Cicero in the Courtroom of St. Thomas Aquinas.* (Marquette University Press, 1946).

396

Rolfe, John C. *Cicero and His Influence.* (Boston, [1923]). (Reprinted New York, 1963.)

397

Spallone, Mario. "La trasmissione della Rhetorica ad Herennium nell'Italia meridionale tra l'XI e il XII secolo." *Bolletino del comitato par la preparazione dell'edizione nazionale dei classici greci e latini, a cura dell'Accademia dei Linei* 1 (1980): 158-90.

398

Zielinski, Tadeusz. *Cicero im Wandel der Jahrhunderte.* 4th ed. (Leipzig, 1929).

II. The Commentary of Thierry of Chartres

399

Delhaye, Philippe. "L'Enseignement de la philosophie morale au XIIᵉ siècle." *MS* 11 (1949): 77-99.

> *Delhaye includes remarks on the use of rhetorical commentaries in classroom teaching, and prints brief excerpts from Thierry of Chartres' commentary on* De inventione.

400

Fredborg, Karin Margareta. "Commentary of Thierry of Chartres on Cicero's 'De inventione.'" *CIMAGL* 7 (1971): 1-37.

> *A discussion of the twelfth century treatise, especially its*

treatment of Argument, which identifies Boethius and Victorinus as major sources, along with the Rhetorica ad Herennium, *Grillius, and Martianus Capella. The author concludes that Dominicus Gundissalinus copied Thierry, and not the other way around. See Haring.*

401

Fredborg, Karin Margareta, ed. *The Latin Rhetorical Commentaries by Thierry of Chartres.* Studies and Texts 84. (Toronto, Leiden, 1988).

Editions of Theodorici Britonis Commentarius super Rhetoricam Ciceronis *(pp. 49-215) and the same author's* Commentarius super Rhetoricam ad Herennium *(pp. 217-361), both apparently written in the 1130's.*

402

Haring, Nicholas M., S.A.C. "Thierry of Chartres and Dominicus Gundissalinus." *MS* 26 (1964): 271-86.

Compares 22 passages in the two works to demonstrate that for his commentary on Cicero's De Inventione *Thierry copied passages on rhetoric from Gundissalinus's* De divisione philosophiae. *For a contrary view see Fredborg.*

III. Other Commentaries

403

Caplan, Harry. "Medieval Commentary on the *Rhetorica ad Herennium.*" In *Of Eloquence.* Ed. Anne King and Helen North. (Cornell University Press, 1970). Pp. 247-270.

Discussion of the twelfth century Latin commentary on the ad Herennium *ascribed in three manuscripts to one "Alanus." Caplan reserves judgment on the question of whether the author might be Alain of Lille.*

404

Dickey, Mary. "Some Commentaries on the *De inventione* and *Ad Herennium* of the Eleventh and Twelfth Centuries." *MARS* 6 (1968): 1-41.

405

Fredborg, Karin Margareta. "Petrus Helias on Rhetoric." *CIMAGL* 13 (1974): 31-41.

Discusses a commentary (c.1130-1139) on Cicero's De inventione by Peter, a student of Thierry of Chartres.

406

Lagorio, Valerie M. "Anonymous Commentary 'De attributis personae et negotio' in Codex Vat. Lat. 3862." *Scriptorium* 31 (1977): 246-7.

407

Ward, John O. "Commentator's Rhetoric: From Antiquity to the Renaissance : Glosses and Commentaries on Cicero's *Rhetorica.*" In *Medieval Eloquence.* Pp. 25-67.

The most comprehensive study of medieval commentaries on Ciceronian rhetoric; includes manuscript listings, frequency charts, and discussions of individual commentaries. See also the continuation of this landmark survey in the Renaissance chapter below.

408

Wertis, Sandra Karaus. "Commentary of Bartolinus de Benincasa de Canulo on the *Rhetorica ad Herennium.*" *Viator* 10 (1979): 283-310.

IV. Vernacular Renderings
Anonymous *Rhetorica ad Herennium*

409

Scolari, Antonio. "Un volgarizzamento trecentesco della *Rhetorica ad Herennium* : il *Trattatello di colori rettorici.*" *Medioevo Romanzo* 9 (1984): 215-266.

Includes text of the Trattatello.

Brunetto Latini: A. Works

410

Carmody, Francis J., ed. *Li Livres dou Tresor.* University of California Publications in Modern Philology 22. (University of California, 1948).

Latini's encyclopedic work, completed about 1260, gives rhetoric a major place.

411

Chabaille, P., ed. *Il Tesoro di Brunetto Latini volgarizzato da Bono Giamboni.* 4 vols. (Bologna, 1878).

This medieval Italian rendering of the Tresor *includes still another version of Latini's basic views on Ciceronian rhetoric.*

412

Holloway, Julia Bottom, ed. and trans. *Il Tesoretto (The Little Treasure).* (New York, 1981).

413

Li livres dou Tresor, III, 60-65. Trans. James R. East. In *Readings.* Pp. 253-264.

The excerpts are from East's 1960 Ph.D. dissertation.

414

Maggini, Francesco, ed. *La Rettorica: Testo Critico.* (Florence, 1915, rpt. 1968).

Brunetto Latini: B. Secondary References

415

Alessio, Gian Carlo. "Brunetto Latini e Cicerone (e i dettatori)." *Italia medioevale e umanistica* 22 (1979): 123-69.

Proposes that Latini used a medieval rhetorical compendium as a source for his Rettorica *and for Book Two of his* Tresor, *rather than using Cicero's works directly.*

416

Baldassarri, Guido. "Ancora sulle 'fonti' della 'Rettorica': Brunetto Latini e Teodorico di Chartres." *Studi e problemi di critica testuale* 19 (1979): 41-69.

417
Murphy, James J. "John Gower's *Confessio amantis* and the First Discussion of Rhetoric in the English Language." *Philological Quarterly* 41 (1962): 401-11.

This article traces the influence of Brunetto Latini's rhetoric on a portion of Gower's work.

418
Ricciardi, Micaela. "Aspetti retorico-stilistici del volgarizzamento della 'Pro Ligario' di Brunetto Latini." *Critica letteraria* 9:2:31 (1981): 266-92.

419
Sgrilli, Paolo. "Retorica e società: tensioni anticlassiche nella 'Retorica' di Brunetto Latini." *Medioevo Romanza* 3 (1976): 380-93.

420
Wieruszowski, Helene. "Brunetto Latini als Lehrer Dantes und der Florentiner." *Archivio italiano per la storia della pietà* 2 (1962): 171-98.

This includes a brief section (186-9) on Brunetto as a teacher of rhetoric in Florence.

Guidotto da Bologna

421
Gamba, Bartolommeo, ed. *Il fiore di rettorica.* (Venice, 1821).

This thirteenth-century Italian treatise is presented by its author as "La elegantissima dottrina dello eccellentissimo Marco Tullio Cicerone."

422
Il fiore di Rettorica (Rettorica nuova di Tullio). Ed. V. Nannuci. Manuale della letteratura del primo secolo della lingua Italiana. 2 vols. (Florence, 1858).

Jean d'Antioche de Harens

423

Delisle, Léopold, ed. "Notice sur la rhétorique de Cicéron traduite par Maître Jean d'Antioche." *Notices et extraits* 36 (1899): 207-65.

> This includes excerpts from Jean's Rettorique de Marc Tulles Ciceron, *a vernacular compendium in six books combining both* De Inventione *and* Rhetorica ad Herennium.

D. Quintilian

424

Boskoff, Priscilla S. "Quintilian in the Late Middle Ages." *Speculum* 27 (1952): 71-8.

425

Brasa Díez, M. "Quintiliano y Juan de Salisbury." *Estudios Filosóficos* 24 (1975): 87-99.

> A study of the Institutio oratorio *in the twelfth century.*

426

Colson, F.H. "Introduction." In *Institutionis oratoriae liber I.* Ed. F.H. Colson. (Cambridge, England, 1924).

> The introduction provides one of the most complete single summaries of the postclassical history of Quintilian's work.

427

Coulter, Cornelia C. "Boccaccio's Knowledge of Quintilian." *Speculum* 33 (1958): 490-96.

428

Erickson, Keith V. "Quintilian's *Institutio oratoria* and Pseudo-Declamationes." [A Bibliography]. *Rhetoric Society Quarterly* 11 (1981): 45-62.

> While this compilation of nearly 1000 items is presented alphabetically by author rather than being organized by subject, it does include many citations dealing with the history of Quintilian's influence over the centuries.

429
Fierville, Charles, ed. *De institutione oratoria liber primus.*
(Paris, 1890).
*Appendix I contains the twelfth-century epitome of book I
written by Etienne de Rouen.*

430
Lehmann, Paul. "Die Institutio oratoria des Quintilianus im Mittelalter." *Philologus* 89 (1934): 349-83. (Reprinted in Paul Lehmann, *Erforschung des Mittelalters*, 4 vols., 2 [Leipzig, 1941-60],
1-28.)

431
Mollard, Auguste. "La Diffusion de l'institution oratoire au XIIe
siècle." *Le moyen âge* 44 (3rd series 5) (1934): 161-75, and 45
(3rd series 6) (1935): 1-9.

432
Mollard, Auguste. "L'Imitation de Quintilien dans Guibert de
Nogent." *Le moyen âge* 44 (3rd series 5) (1934): 81-7.

433
Seel, Otto. *Quintilian, oder die Kunst des Redens und Schweigens.*
(Stuttgart, 1977).
*Includes (pp. 161-325) a survey of Quintilian's influence down
into modern times.*

E. John of Salisbury: Works

434
McGarry, Daniel D., trans. *Metalogicon of John of Salisbury.*
(University of California Press, 1955).

435
Webb, Clemens C.H., ed. *Metalogicon.* (Oxford, 1929).
*This is an extremely important text (1159) which shows in
books I-II the twelfth-century influence of humanism in the
tradition of Quintilian and in books III-IV the impact of two
newly translated Aristotelian logical works which became the*

basis for the dialectical disputations of the universities.

E. John of Salisbury: Secondary References

436

Brasa Díez, M. "Las artes del lenguaje en Juan de Salisbury." *La Ciudad de Dios* 193 (1980): 19-45.

437

Martel, Jean-Paul. "Rhétorique et philosophie dans le 'Metalogicon' de Jean de Salisbury." Vol. 2 of *In Actas del V Congreso internacional de filosofía medieval.* (Madrid, 1979).

438

Tacchella, Enrico. "Giovanni di Salisbury e i Cornificiani." *Sandalion* 3 (1980): 273-313.

439

von Moos, Peter. *Geschichte als Topik: Das rhetorische Exemplum von der Antike zur Neuzeit und die Historiae* im *Polycraticus* Johanns von Salisbury. (Hildesheim, 1988).

F. Miscellaneous Works and References

440

Alain of Lille. *Anticlaudian of Alain de Lille, Prologue, Argument and Nine Books.* Trans. William H. Cornog. (Philadelphia, 1935). *Rhetoric is one of the seven young ladies representing the liberal arts in this allegorical work written about 1184.*

441

Henri d'Andeli. *Battle of the Seven Arts: A French Poem by Henri d'Andeli, Trouvère of the Thirteenth Century.* Part I of *Two Medieval Satires on the University of Paris.* Ed. and trans. Louis J. Paetow. Memoirs of the University of California 4, part I. (University of California Press, 1914).

442
Zinn, G.A. "Hugh of St. Victor and The Art of Memory." *Viator* 5 (1974): 211-234.

IV
Letter Writing:
Ars dictaminis

The *ars dictaminis*, applying Roman rhetorical principles to the art of composing letters, has been called "a truly medieval invention." In recent years there has been controversy over the origins of the art; some (e.g. Patt, Lanham) have argued that letter-writing practice in Europe was shaped along the lines of *dictamen* long before there were any theoretical treatises (*artes*) to prescribe the process; others (e.g. Murphy, Gehl) point to the first formal treatises in the 1080's as the genesis of the art. In any case it does seem clear that the first written manuals are products of the late eleventh century, associated with the Benedictine monastery of Monte Cassino in central Italy; the lore then spreads to Rome and the Curia; Bologna and Florence were its chief municipal centers during the twelfth century. By 1135 the basic doctrines had been clearly spelled out and remained substantially unchanged for four centuries. Famous Italian *dicatores* like Guido Faba and Buoncompagno were known all over Europe.

Essentially the *ars dictaminis* applied Ciceronian rhetorical principles to letter-writing. A five-part letter format was developed. In a hierarchical society extreme importance was of course attached to the social level of both letter-writer and addressee—a concern which resulted in complex theories of salutation level and stylistic variation. A special rhythmical prose style—the *cursus*—was also a feature of the art.

Along with preceptive manuals (*artes dictaminis*) which described how to write letters, the movement results in numerous collections of formularies and model letters (*dictamina*) for verbatim copying by those unable or unwilling to prepare letters of their own. In some cases, especially late in the middle ages, this formula-copying tendency merged into the area of legal documentation so that the history of the *ars notaria* also has a bearing on the subject.

Finally, it should be noted that there has been recent interest in the relation between *dictamen* and humanism in the late middle ages and early Renaissance (e.g. Witt, Siegel, Kristeller in Chapter 9, Renaissance).

A. History: Eight Basic Studies

443
Constable, Giles. *Letters and Letter-Collections.* Typologie des sources du moyen âge occidental, 17. (Turnhout, 1976).

> *A masterful study of the medieval "letter" as a genre, though the author is naturally enough interested primarily in letters* per se *rather than being concerned with their rhetorical aspects.*

444

de Ghellinck, Joseph. *L'Essor de la littérature latine au XIIe siècle.* 2 vols. (Brussels and Paris, 1946).

> *This includes a good brief survey (pp. 54-68) of the development of* dictamen, *especially in France.*

445

Denholm-Young, Noel. "*Cursus* in England." In *Collected Papers of N. Denholm-Young.* (Cardiff, 1969). Pp. 42-73.

> *In this excellent short survey of the* ars dictaminis *and cursus, or rhythmical prose style, Denholm-Young provides an appendix listing English manuscript holdings of thirty-two dictaminal authors, with biographical data where known, and an important alphabetical list of incipits which is indispensable to any serious study of the subject. This article first appeared in* Oxford Essays in Medieval History Presented to Herbert Edward Salter *(Oxford, 1934), 68-103.*

446

Haskins, Charles H. "Early *Artes dictandi* in Italy." In *Studies in Mediaeval Culture.* (Oxford, 1929). Pp. 170-92.

> *One of the most important single historical treatments in English, it covers the initial development of the* ars dictaminis *from Alberic of Monte Cassino (1087) to about 1150.*

447

Murphy, James J. "*Ars dictaminis*: The Art of Letter-Writing." In *Rhetoric in the Middle Ages.* Pp. 194-268.

> *Traces the development of theories of letter-writing from late antiquity to the emergence of the rival* ars notaria, *with discussions of early medieval formularies and the appearance of formal* artes dictaminis; *includes treatment of major authors.*

448

Schmale, Franz-Josef. "Die Bologneser Schule der Ars dictandi." *Deutsches Archiv für Erforschung des Mittelalters* 13 (1957): 16-34.

> *This discussion of relations between the anonymous* Aurea gemma, Aurea gemma Willelmi, De dictamine, *a Lombard tract, and other Bolognese dictaminal works is over-detailed as*

a first reading on the subject, but provides illuminating background to the sketch of Haskins.

449
Valois, Noël. *De arte scribendi epistolas apud Gallicos medii aevi scriptores rhetoresve.* (Paris, 1880).
This Latin treatise is limited in scope, largely because Valois deals almost exclusively with manuscripts readily available to him in Paris.

450
Vecchi, Giuseppe. *Il magistero delle "Artes" latine a Bologna nel medioevo.* Pubblicazioni della facoltà di Magistero Università di Bologna 2. (Bologna, [1958]).
An important brief study of trends in the Bolognese dictaminal movement, it includes a précis of Bene of Florence's Candelabrum, *showing Bene's relation to Geoffrey of Vinsauf.*

B. General Studies

451
Capua, Francesco di. *Sentenze e proverbi nella tecnica oratoria e loro influenze sull'arte del periodare.* Studi sulla letteratura latina medievale. (Naples, 1947).

452
Constable, Giles. "Structure of Medieval Society According to the *Dictatores* of the Twelfth Century." In *Law, Church, and Society: Essays in Honor of Stephan Kuttner.* Ed. Kenneth Pennington and Robert Sommerville. (University of Pennsylvania Press, 1977). Pp. 253-67.

453
Fichtenau, Heinrich. *Arenga: Spätantike und Mittelalter im Spiegel von Urkundenformeln.* MIÖG. Ergänzungsband 18. (1957).

454

Gaudenzi, Augusto. "Sulla cronologia delle opere dei dettatori Bolognesi da Buoncompagno a Bene di Lucca." *Bullettino dell'istituto storico italiano* 14 (1895): 85-174.

455

Gehl, Paul F. "From Monastic Rhetoric to *Ars dictaminis*: Traditionalism and Innovation in the Schools of Twelfth-Century Italy." *The American Benedictine Review* 34 (1983): 33-47.

456

Giry, Arthur. *Manuel de diplomatique*. 2 vols. new ed. (Paris, 1925).

> *Giry has a short treatment of the Papal* cursus, *uses of* formulae *up to the eleventh century, and the* ars dictaminis *itself. He is one of the few writers who has even a brief comment on the relation of formularies to the* ars dictaminis.

457

Haskins, Charles H. "Life of Medieval Students as Illustrated by Their Letters." In *Studies in Mediaeval Culture*. (Oxford, 1929). Pp. 1-35.

> *This provides an interesting companion to Haskins' systematic historical survey published in the same volume.*

458

La Lexicographie du latin médiéval et ses rapports avec les recherches actuelles sur la civilisation du Moyen -Age. Actes du colloque international, Paris, 18-21 Octobre, 1978. Colloques internationaux du Centre national de la recherche scientifique, No. 589. (Paris, 1981).

459

Lawton, David A. "Gaytryge's Sermon, *Dictamen*, and Middle English Alliterative Verse." *Modern Philology* 76 (1979): 329-43.

460

Leclercq, Jean. "Le Genre épistolaire au moyen âge." *Revue du moyen âge latin* 2 (1946): 63-70.

> *An eloquent plea for continued study of the genre.*

461
Leclercq, Jean. "Sancta simplicitas." *Collectanea ordinis Cisterciensium reformatorum* 22 (1960): 138-48.

In this perceptive article Leclercq distinguishes a basic conflict between Christian humility and certain types of stylistic extravagance found in pagan rhetoric.

462
Patt, William D. "Early *Ars dictaminis* as Response to a Changing Society." *Viator* 9 (1978): 133-55.

Argues that letter-writing practices were standardized long before Alberic of Monte Cassino's two works, and that therefore Alberic could not have originated the ars dictaminis.

463
Polak, Emil J. "Dictamen." In *A Dictionary of the Middle Ages.* Ed. Joseph R. Strayer. 13 vols. (New York, 1982-). Vol. 4 (1984), 173-177.

464
Polak, Emil J. "Latin Epistolography of the Middle Ages and Renaissance: Manuscript Evidence in Poland." *Eos* 73 (1985): 349-362.

465
Richardson, Henry Gerald. "Business Training in Medieval Oxford." *American Historical Review* 46 (1941): 259-80.

466
Rockinger, Ludwig. *Über Briefsteller und Formelbücher in Deutschland während des Mittelalters.* (Munich, 1861).

A pioneering study which culminated two years later in Rockinger's landmark collection of texts (1863).

467
Schaller, Hans Martin. "Ars dictaminis, Ars dictandi." In *Verfasser Lexikon des Mittelalters.* (Munich, 1980-). I (1980), 1034-1039.

468
Vecchi, Giuseppe. "Il 'proverbio' nella pratica letteraria dei dettatori della scuola di Bologna." *Studi mediolatini e volgari* 2 (1954):

283-302.
The use of proverbs in letters was frequently recommended by the dictaminal manuals.

469
Wieruszowski, Helene. "Arezzo as a Center of Learning and Letters in the Thirteenth Century." *Traditio* 9 (1953): 321-91.

470
Wieruszowski, Helene. "*Ars dictaminis* in the Time of Dante." *Medievalia et Humanistica* 1 (1943): 95-108.

471
Wieruszowski, Helene. "Rhetoric and the Classics in Italian Education of the Thirteenth Century." *Studia Gratiana* 11 (1967): 169-208.

472
Worstbrock, Franz J. "Die Antikenrezeption in der mittelalterlichen und der humanistischen 'Ars dictandi.'" In *Die Rezeption der Antike: Zum Problem der Koutinuität zwischen Mittelalter und Renaissance.* Ed. Augustus Buck. Wolfenbütteler Abhandlungen zur Renaissance-Forschungen, I. (Hamburg, 1981). Pp. 187-207.

C. Authors and Works

A. Collection

473
Rockinger, Ludwig. *Briefsteller und Formelbücher des eilften bis vierzehnten Jahrhunderts.* Quellen und Erörterungen zur bayerischen und deutschen Geschichte 9. (Munich, 1863). (Reprinted in two volumes with continuous pagination, New York, 1961.)
This fundamental work contains the following texts, summaries, and descriptions (the Roman numerals are Rockinger's):
I   *Introduction*
II   *Alberic of Monte Cassino*

A Rationes dictandi (*not Alberic's: see Haskins [1929]*).

 B [Breviarum] de dictamine

III *Hugh of Bologna*, Rationes dictandi prosaice

IV *Anonymous*, Ars dictandi aurelianensis

V *Boncompagno of Florence*
  A Cedrus
  B Boncompagnus (*summary*)

VI *Guido Faba*
  A Doctrina ad inueniendas incipiendas et formandas materias et ad ea que circa huiusmodi requiruntur
  B* Doctrina priuilegiorum

VII *Anonymous*, Summa prosarum dictaminis

VIII *Ludolf of Hildesheim*, Summa dictaminum

IX *Konrad of Mure*, Summa de arte prosandi

X *"Johannes anglicus"* [*John of Garland*], Poetria magistri Johannis anglici de arte prosayca metrica et rithmica (*summary with excerpts*)

XI *Dominicus Dominici of Viseu*, Summa dictaminis secundum quod notarii episcoporum et archyepiscoporum debeant officium exercere

XII* *John of Bologna*, Summa notarie

XIII* *Anonymous*, Formularius de modo prosandi

XIV *Bernold of Kaisersheim*, Summula dictaminis

XV* *Anonymous*, Formeln für Rechtsgeschäfte

XVI *"Johannes Bondi"* [*Lawrence?*] *of Aquilegia*, Practica siue dictaminis

XVII *Master Simon*, Notabilia . . . super summa de arte dictandi

XVIII *Anonymous*, Summa de ordine et processu iudicii spiritualis

XIX *An alphabetical list of formulary incipits*

XX *Index*

This basic collection of texts is absolutely indispensable for a study of the ars dictaminis. *However, Rockinger's introduction is not especially useful. It should be noted that a number of his texts are not true* artes dictaminis *that deal with the theory of letter-writing but are instead collections of model letters or formularies; these are marked with an asterisk:* VI (B), XII, XIII, XV. *And it should also be noted that Rockinger does not always print the complete text of some works. The* Rationes dictandi *(pp. 9-28) attributed by Rockinger to Alberic of Monte Cassino is clearly not Alberic's.*

Adalbertus Samaritanus

474

Schmale, Franz-Josef, ed. *Praecepta dictaminum.* MGH, Quellen zur Geistesgeschichte des Mittelalters 3. (Weimar, 1961).

Alberic of Monte Cassino: A. Works

475.

Davis, Hugh H. "'De rithmis' of Alberic of Monte Cassino: A Critical Edition." *MS* 28 (1966): 198-227.

> *The text is on pp. 208-14.*

476

Flowers of Rhetoric. Trans. Joseph M. Miller. In *Readings.* Pp. 132-61.

> *Translation of* Flores rhetorici *(or* Dictaminum radii*) from the edition of Inguanez and Willard.*

477

Inguanez, D.M. and H.M. Willard, eds. *Flores rhetorici.* Miscellanea Cassinese 14. (Monte Cassino, 1938).

> *Hagendahl asserts that its proper title should be* Dictaminum radii *(found in three manuscripts) rather than* Flores rhetorici *as found in only one manuscript.*

478

Rockinger, Ludwig, ed. *Breviarium de dictamine.* In *Briefsteller und Formelbücher des eilften bis vierzehnten Jahrhunderts.* Quellen und Erörterungen zur bayerischen und deutschen Geschichte 9. (Munich, 1863). (Reprinted in two volumes with continuous pagination, New York, 1961.)

> *This very early treatise indicates that the basic doctrines of the* ars dictaminis *were shaped at Monte Cassino by the 1080s or 90s.*

Alberic of Monte Cassino: B. Secondary References

479

Bloch, H. "Monte Cassino's Teachers and Library in the High Middle Ages." Vol. 19 of *La scuola nell'occidente latino dell'alto medioevo.* Settimane di studio del Centro Italiano di studi sull'alto medioevo. (Spoleto, 1972).

> *Defends nomination of Alberic of Montecassino as earliest theorist of* ars dictaminis.

480

Hagendahl, Harald. "Le Manuel de rhétorique d'Albericus Casinensis." *Classica et Medievalia* 17 (1956): 63-70.

481

Holtz, Louis. "Le Parisinus Latinus 7530, synthèse cassinienne des arts libéraux." *Studi Medievali* 16 (1975): 97-152.

> *Discussion of Paris B.N. Ms. Lat 7530 (dated 779-796) as evidence of a systematic teaching program at Montecassino.*

Anonymous

482

Pantin, William A., ed. "Medieval Treatise on Letter-writing, with Examples, from the Rylands Latin MS 394." *Bulletin of*

the John Rylands Library 13 (1929): 326-82.
Perhaps this is to be attributed to "Simon O."
483
Schmale, Franz-Josef, ed. *Die Precepta prosaici dictaminis secundum Tullium und die Konstanzer Briefsammlung.* (Bonn, 1950).

Anonymous Halberstadt 'ars dictandi'
484
Zöllner, Walter. "Die Halberstädter Ars dictandi aus den Jahren 1193-94." *Wissenschaftliche Zeitschrift der Halberstadter Universität* 13 (1964): 539-56.

Anonymous Italian 'ars dictaminis'
485
Dursza, Sándor. "L'ars dictaminis di un maestro italiano del secolo XII." *Acta Literaria Academiae Scientiarum Hungaricae* (Budapest) 12 (1970): 159-73.

Anonymous 'compendium'
486
Dursza, Sándor. "Compendium Rhetoricae Venustatis." *Filológiai Közlöny* 20 (Budapest, 1974): 299-305.
   Discusses an Ars dictandi, accompanied by a collection of salutationes, in a Budapest manuscript. The author compares the ars with the works of Guido Faba.

Anonymous of Bologna

487
Principles of Letter-writing (Rationes Dictandi). Trans. James
J. Murphy. In *Three Medieval Rhetorical Arts.* Ed. James J.
Murphy. (University of California Press, 1971). Pp. 5-25.
> *This treatise, written in 1135 by an anonymous author of
> Bologna, lays out a five-part "approved format" that
> became standard in medieval dictaminal theory.*

Anonymous 'rhetorica ecclesiastica'

488
Wahrmund, Ludwig, ed. *Die Rhetorica ecclesiastica.* Quellen
zur Geschichte des römisch-kanonischen Prozesses im Mittelalter 1, Heft 4. (Innsbruck, 1906).
> *The author of the treatise (c. 1160-80) declares (p.2) his
> intention to teach canon law partly through* artificiosam
> doctrinam rhetorum.

Baldwin

489
Dursza, Sándor. "Il liber dictaminum di Baldwinus." *Quadrivium* 13 (1972): 5-41.
> *See also J. Loserth.*

Baldwin of Viktring

490
Schaller, Dieter. "Baldwin von Viktring. Zisterziensische ars
dictaminis im 12. Jahrhundert." *Deutsches Archiv für
Erforschung des Mittelalters* 35 (1979): 127-37.
> *Discusses a twelfth century* Liber dictaminum *written espe-
> cially for monastic use.*

Bene of Florence: A. Works

491

Alessio, Gian Carlo, ed. *Bene Florentini Candelabrum.* (Padua, 1983).

> *Edition of this important text, heretofore available only in fragments or paraphrases.*

492

Vecchi, Giuseppe. "Temi e momenti d'arte dettatoria nel 'Candelabrum' di Bene da Firenze." *Atti e memorie della Deputazione di storia patria per le province di Romagna* 10 (1958/59): 113-68.

> *Includes an edition of the fifth book of the* Candelabrum.

Bene of Florence: B. Secondary References

493

Alessio, Gian Carlo. "La Tradizione manoscritta del 'Candelabrum' di Bene da Firenze." *Medioevo romanzo* 15 (1972): 99-148.

Bernard

494

Haskins, Charles H. "Italian Master Bernard." In *Essays in History Presented to Reginald Lane Poole.* Ed. Henry W.C. Davis. (Oxford, 1927). Pp. 211-26.

Bernard of Meung: A. Works

495

Delisle, Léopold, ed. "Notice sur une 'Summa dictaminis' jadis conservée à Beauvais." *Notices et extraits* 36 (1899): 171-205.

> *The text is that of Bernard of Meung, popular writer in the Orleanistic tradition, and includes a section on the* cursus.

The dictaminal writers of Orléans tended to be more humanistic than the Italians. For a formulary by Bernard see Auvray.

496
Vulliez, Charles. "Un nouveau manuscrit 'parisien' de la 'Summa dictaminis' de Bernard de Meung et sa place dans la tradition manuscrite du texte." *Revue d' histoire des textes* 7 (1977): 133-51.

497
Zöllner, Walter, ed. "Eine neue Bearbeitung der 'Flores dictaminum' des Bernhard von Meung." *Wissenschaftliche Zeitschrift der Martin-Luther-Universität Halle-Wittenberg: Gesellschafts- und sprachwissenschaftliche Reihe* 13, Heft 5 (1964): 335-42.

Bernard of Meung: B. Secondary References

498
Camargo, Martin. "English Manuscripts of Bernard of Meung's *Flores dictaminum*." *Viator* 12 (1981): 197-219.

Bernardus Silvestris

499
Savorelli, M. Brini. "Il *Dictamen* di Bernardo Silvestre." *Rivista critica di storia della filosofia* 20 (1965): 182-230.
    Text of Summa dictaminis magistri Bernardi *(pp. 201-230) from a Viennese manuscript.*

Bichilino da Spello

500
Licitra, Vincenzo, ed. *Il 'Pomerium rethorice' di Bichilino da Spello*. Quaderni del "Centro per il collegamento degli studi medievali e umanistici nell'Università di Perugia," 5.

(Florence, 1979).
An ars dictandi *with letter collection.*

Boncompagno

501

Gaudenzi, Augusto, ed. *Rhetorica novissima.* In *Bibliotheca iuridica medii aevi, scripta anecdota glossatorum* 2. (Bologna, 1892). Pp. 249-97.

> *Baldwin and Paetow have accounts of this boastful Bolognese* dictator, *who once wrote that Cicero was not worth his attention, and who advertised the work cited here as the final word on rhetoric; but actually he had little influence. Paetow, for instance, greatly magnifies his importance.*

502

Purkart, Josef, ed. *Rota veneris: A Facsimile Reproduction of the Stassburg Incunabulum with Introduction, Translation, and Notes.* Scholars' Facsimiles and Reprints. (Delmar, New York, 1975).

> *Purkhart describes the* Rota veneris *as a "summa dictaminis de arte amandi," mixing rhetorical lore with literary eroticism.*

503

Sutter, Carl, ed. *Aus Leben und Schriften des Magisters Boncompagno.* (Freiburg im Breisgau and Leipzig, 1894).

> *This contains an edition of his* Palma, *pp.105-27.*

504

Witt, Ronald. "Boncompagno and the Defense of Rhetoric." *The Journal of Medieval and Renaissance Studies* 16 (1986): 1-31.

Brunetto Latini

505
East, James Robert. "Brunetto Latini's Rhetoric of Letter Writing." *QJS* 54 (1968): 241-6.
> *East discusses the way in which Latini adapted Ciceronian rhetoric to both speaking and letter-writing.*

Gaufridus

506
Worstbrock, Franz Josef. "Zu Galfrids *Summa de arte dictandi.*" *Deutsches Archiv für Erforschung des Mittelalters* 23 (1967): 549-552.

Gaufridus Anglicus

507
Pizzorusso, Valeria Bertolucci. "Un trattato di *Ars dictandi* dedicato ad Alfonso X." *Studio mediolatino e volgari* 15 (1967): 3-82.
> *Discusses the* Ars epistolaris ornatus *of Gaufridus Anglicus with text (pp. 59-82) from the unique Biblioteca Communale Augusta di Perugia MS F.62.*

Giovanni del Virgilio

508
Billanovich, Giuseppe. "Giovanni del Virgilio, Pietro da Moglio, Francesco da Fiano." *Italia medioevale e umanistica* 6 (1963): 203-234; and 7 (1964), 279-324.

509
Kristeller, Paul O., ed. "Un 'Ars dictaminis' di Giovanni del Virgilio." *Italia medioevale e umanistica* 4 (1961): 181-200.
> *Kristeller presents the text (pp.193-200) of a treatise written before 1327.*

Giovanni di Bonandrea

510

Banker, James R. "*Ars dictaminis* and Rhetorical Textbooks at the Bolognese University in the Fourteenth Century." *Medievalia et Humanistica* N.S. 5 (1974): 153-68.

Argues that the Brevis introductio ad dictaminam *of Giovanni di Bonandrea was the dominant dictaminal text in the period 1325-1400, and was coupled with lectures on the* Rhetorica ad Herennium *for students of the* ars oratoria.

511

Banker, James R. "Giovanni di Bonandrea and Civic Values in the Context of the Italian Rhetorical Tradition." *Manuscripta* 18 (1974): 3-20.

512

Zaccagnini, Guido. "Giovanni di Bonandrea dettatore e rimatore e altri grammatici e dottori in arti dello studio Bolognese." *Studi e memorie per la storia dell' Università di Bologna* 5 (1920): 145-204.

It includes extracts (pp.191-4) from the Summa dictaminis *of Giovanni (fl. 1269-1303).*

Guido Faba: A. Works

513

Chirico, Lina, ed. "Un trattato inedito di Guido Fava." *Biblion rivista di bibliofilia e di erudizione varia* 1 (1946-47): 227-34.

514

Gaudenzi, Augusto, ed. "*Summa dictaminis.*" *Il Propugnatore* 23 (NS 3) (1890): I, 287-338 and II, 345-93.

515

Pini, Virgilio, ed. "La *Summa de vitiis et virtutibus* di Guido Faba." *Quadrivium* 1 (1956): 41-152.

The text is on pp.97-152 with exordia *in Latin and Italian.*

Pini also lists (pp.42-43) editions of Guido Faba's other works.

Guido Faba: B. Secondary References

516
Faulhaber, Charles B. "Letter-Writer's Rhetoric: The *Summa dictaminis* of Guido Faba." In *Medieval Eloquence*. Pp. 85-111.

517
Kantorowicz, Ernst H. "'Autobiography' of Guido Faba." *MARS* 1 (1941): 253-80.
In addition to an interesting survey to this popular dictator*'s career, Kantorowicz includes the prologue to Faba's unedited* Rota nova.

Henricus de Isernia

518
Tříška, Josef. "Prague Rhetoric and the *Epistolare dictamen* (1278) of Henricus de Isernia." *Rhetorica* 3 (1985): 183-200.
Includes text (pp.192-198) of prologue to the Epistolare dictamen.

Jacques of Dinant

519
Polak, Emil J. *Textual Study of Jacques de Dinant's Summa dictaminis*. Études de philologie et d'histoire, 28. (Geneva, 1975).
Includes an edition of the Summa.

520
Wilmart, André, ed. *Ars arengandi*. In *Analecta reginensia: Studi e testi* 59. (Vatican City, 1933). Pp. 113-51.
This treatise shows clear influence of the pseudo-

Ciceronian Rhetorica ad Herennium.

John of Limoges

521

Horváth, Constantine, ed. *Libellus de dictamine et dictatorio syllogismorum.* Vol. 1 of *Johannis Lemovicensis opera omnia.* 3 vols. (Veszprém, 1932). Pp. 1-69.

John was a Cistercian abbot of Zirc, 1208-18. The Cistercians were frequent composers of dictaminal manuals.

Laurence of Aquilegia

522

Capdevila, S. "La 'Practica dictaminis' de Llorens de Aquileia, en un còdex de Tarragona." *Analecta sacra Tarraconensia* 6 (1930): 207-29.

An edition of the Practica.

Matteo dei Libri

523

Vincenti, Eleonora, ed. *Arringhe.* Documenti di Filologia, 19. (Milan, 1974).

Peter of Blois

524

Camargo, Martin. "*Libellus de arte dictandi rhetorice* Attributed to Peter of Blois." *Speculum* 59 (1984): 16-41.

A detailed discussion of the Libellus, *including a summary of the arguments against Peter's authorship, and the treatise beginning* Floribus rhetoricis, *concluding that the "uniqueness" of both texts prevented them from becoming standard texts.*

Pons of Provence

525

Fierville, Charles, ed. *Une grammaire latine inédite du XIIIe siècle.* (Paris, 1886).

This volume has excerpts from the De dictamine *of Pons, as well as the text of* De metrico dictamine. *The* De dictamine *was one of the very few medieval dictaminal manuals to be printed during the fifteenth century, appearing as* Rethorica Poncii *(Strassburg, 1486).*

Thomas of Capua

526

Heller, Emmy, ed. *Die Ars dictandi des Thomas von Capua.* Sitzungsberichte der Heidelberger Akademie der Wissenschaften, philosophisch-historische Klasse, Jahrgang 1928-9: 4. Abhandlung. (Heidelberg, 1929).

Tommasino of Armannino

527

Bertoni, Giulio. "Il 'Microcosmo' di Tommasino d'Armannino." *Archivum Romanicum* 5 (1921): 19-28.

Edition of Microcosmus (Summa dictaminis) *of Tommasino.*

Ventura da Bergamo

528

Thomson, David and James J. Murphy. "Dictamen as a Developed Genre: The Fourteenth Century *Brevis doctrina dictaminis* of Ventura da Bergamo." *Studi medievali* Third series, 23 (1982): 361-86.

The edition of this text is presented as an example of a typical or standard dictaminal treatise; one unique feature of the Brevis doctrina, *however, is a section on scribal abbreviations to be used in writing letters.*

William

529

Samaran, Charles, ed. "Une *Summa grammaticalis* du XIIIe siècle avec gloses provençales." *Archivum latinitatis medii aevi (Bulletin du Cange)* 31 (1961): 157-224.

This is an edition of the Summa de dictamine; *the treatise (c. 1218) is presented by Master William as part of a three-part* Summa *which also includes a part called* De declinatione *and another titled* De regimine (dictionis). *This joining of the* dictamen *to the grammatical lore is typical of French writers of the period.*

D. Rhythmical Prose Style *(Cursus)*

530

Capua, Francesco di. *Fonti ed esempi per lo studio dello "stilus curiae romanae" medioevale.* Testi medioevali 3. (Rome, 1941).

531

Capua, Francesco di. *Il ritmo prosaico nelle lettere dei papi e nei documenti della cancellaria romana dal IV al XIV secolo.* 3 vols. (Rome, 1937-46).

532

Capua, Francesco di. *Insegnamenti retorici medievali e dottrine estetiche moderne nel 'De vulgari eloquentia' di Dante.* (Naples, 1945).

533

Clark, Albert C. *Cursus in Mediaeval and Vulgar Latin.* (Oxford, 1910).

534
Clark, Albert C. *Fontes prosae numerosae.* (Oxford, 1909).
This presents an excellent selection of texts illustrative of the cursus.

535
Clark, Albert C. *Prose Rhythm in English.* (Oxford, 1913).

536
Couture, Léonce. "Le 'Cursus' ou rythme prosaïque dans la liturgie et la littérature de l'église latine du IIIᵉ siècle à la renaissance." *Revue des questions historiques* 51 (NS 7) (1892): 253-61.

537
Duchesne, L'abbé. "Note sur l'origine du 'cursus' ou rythme prosaïque suivi dans la rédaction des bulles pontificales." *Bibliothèque de l'école des Chartes* 50 (1889): 161-3.

538
Meyer, Wilhelm. "Die rythmische lateinische Prosa." Vol. 2 of *Gesammelte Abhandlungen zur mittellateinischen Rhythmik.* 3 vols. (Berlin, 1905-36).
This collected work has other material on rhythmical prose.

539
Nicolau, Mathieu G. *L'Origine du "cursus" rythmique et les débuts de l'accent d'intensité en latin.* (Paris, 1930).
This is an influential study of the rationale for the cursus.

540
Polheim, Karl. *Die lateinische Reimprosa.* (Berlin, 1963).

541
Poole, Reginald L. *Lectures on the History of the Papal Chancery, down to the Time of Innocent III.* (Cambridge University Press, 1915).
This is an important study (esp. pp. 83ff.) of the development of the papal cursus *under Pope Gelasius II in the early twelfth century.*

542

Ronconi, Alessandro. "Il 'cursus' medievale e il testo di Cicerone." *Studi italiani di filologia classica* 11 (1934): 99-120.

543

Schiaffini, Alfredo. "La tecnica della 'prose rimata' nel medioevo latino, in Guido Faba, Guittone e Dante." *Studi romanzi* 21 (1931): 7-115.

544

Toynbee, Paget J. "Bearing of the *Cursus* on the Text of Dante's *De vulgari eloquentia.*" *PBA* 10 (1923): 359-77.

> *Toynbee's article is especially valuable for a brief section outlining the complexities of the three main types of the* cursus. *It also appeared in* The Letters of Dante: Emended Text, with Introduction, Translation, Notes and Indices and Appendix on the Cursus, *ed. Paget Toynbee (Oxford, 1920), 244-7; a second edition appeared in 1966.*

545

Valois, Noël. "Etude sur le rythme des bulles pontificales." *Bibliothèque de l'ecole des Chartres* 42 (1881): 161-98, 257-72.

546

Witt, Ronald. "On Bene of Florence's Conception of the French and Roman *Cursus.*" *Rhetorica* 3 (1985): 77-98.

E. Dictaminal Formularies and Letter Collections *(Dictamina)*

547

Auvray, Lucien. *Documents orléanais du XIIe et du XIIIe siècle : extraits du formulaire de Bernard de Meung.* (Orléans, 1892).

548

Baerwald, Hermann, ed. *Das Baumgartenberger Formelbuch.* Fontes rerum austriacarum, Oesterreichische Geschichts-Quellen 25, part II. (Vienna, 1866).

549

Bagliani, Agostino Paravicini. "Eine Briefsammlung für Rektoren des Kirchenstaates (1250-1320)." *Deutsches Archiv für Erforschung des Mittelalters* 35 (1979): 138-208.

550

Beyer, Heinz-Jurgen. Die 'Aurea Gemma': Ihr Verhältnis zu den frühen Artes dictandi. (Diss. Bochum, 1973).

Argues that a common model, depending in part on the Praecepta dictaminum *of Aldalbertus Samaritanus, underlies the various versions of the collection of model letters known as* Aurea gemma.

551

Cartellieri, Alexander. *Ein Donaueschinger Briefsteller: Lateinische Stilübungen des XII. Jahrhunderts aus der Orléans'schen Schule.* (Innsbruck, 1898).

552

Delisle, Léopold. "Des recueils épistolaires de Bérard de Naples." *Notices et extraits* 27, part II (1879): 87-149.

553

Delisle, Léopold. "Le Formulaire de Tréguier et les écoliers bretons des écoles d'Orléans au commencement du XIVe siècle." *Mémoires de la société archéologique et historique de l'Orléans* 23 (1892): 41-64.

This work was also issued separately at Orléans in 1890.

554

Erdmann, Carl, and Norbert Fickermann, eds. *Briefsammlungen der Zeit Heinrichs IV.* MGH, Briefe, 5. (Weimar, 1950).

555

Fisher, John H. "Chancery Standard and Modern Written English." *Journal of the Society of Archivists* 6 (1979): 136-44.

556

Fohlen, Jeannine. "Un apocryphe de Sénèque mal connu: le 'De uerborum copia.'" *MS* 42 (1980): 139-211.

Edition of the ninth letter of the apocryphal correspondence of Seneca and St. Paul.

557

Guido Faba. *Dictamina rhetorica.* Ed. Augusto Gaudenzi. In *Il Propugnatore.* 25, N.S. (1892), I, 86-129 and II, 58-109. [Note: For his *Epistole*, ed. Augusto Gaudenzi, see *Il Propugnatore* 26, NS 6 (1893), I, 359-90 and II, 373-89].

> *As the title indicates, this is a collection of* dictamina— *i.e., model letters—and not a treatise on how to write letters. Guido's was one of the most popular collections.*

558

Haskins, Charles H. "Early Bolognese Formulary." In *Mélanges d'histoire offerts à Henri Pirenne.* (Brussels, 1926). Pp. 201-10.

559

Holtzmann, Walther. "Eine oberitalienische *Ars dictandi* und die Briefsammlung des Priors Peter von St. Jean in Sens." *Neues Archiv 46* (1926): 34-52.

560

Kaeppeli, Tommaso. "Corrispondenza domenicana dell' *Ars dictaminis* di Bartolomeo da Faenza e in formulario anonimo." *AFP* 21 (1951): 228-71.

561

Kantorowicz, Ernst H. "Anonymi 'Aurea Gemma.'" *Medievalia et Humanistica* 1 (1943): 41-57.

562

Kantorowicz, Ernst H. "Petrus de Vinea in England." *MIÖG* 51 (1937): 43-88.

> *Peter of Vinea's collection of model letters was very popular, and this article by Kantorowicz might well serve as an exemplar of studies of this type. It should be compared to the same author's research on the career of Guido Faba.*

563

Koch, Walter. "Zu Sprache, Stil und Arbeitstechnik in den Diplomen Friedrich Barbarossas." *MIÖG* 88 (1980): 36-69.

> *Includes a survey of the influence of various elements,*

including rhetoric, on diplomatics.

564
Ladner, Gerhart. "Formularbehelfe in der Kanzlei Kaiser Friedrichs II. und die 'Briefe des Petrus de Vinea.'" *MIÖG.* Ergänzungsband 12, Heft 1 (1932): 92-198.

565
Langlois, Charles V. "Formulaires de lettres du XIIe, du XIIIe, et du XIVe siècle." *Notices et extraits* 34, part I (1891): 1-32 and 305-22; 34, part II (1895): 1-18 and 19-29; 35, part II (1897): 409-34 and 793-830.

566
Löfstedt, Bengt, and Carol D. Lanham. "Zu den neugefundenen Salzburger Formelbüchern und Briefen." *Eranos* 73 (1975): 69-100.
 The manuscript discussed dates from the Carolingian period.

567
Loserth, J. "Formularbücher der Grazer Universitätsbibliothek." *Neues Archiv* 21 (1895-96): 307-11; 22 (1896-97): 299-307; 23 (1897-98), 751-61.
 Loserth includes a description of Liber Baldwini de dictaminibus *(c. 1147-61) which is mentioned by Haskins.*

568
Plechl, Helmut. "Studien zur Tegernseer Briefsammlung des 12. Jahrhunderts." *Deutsches Archiv für Erforschung des Mittelalters* part I: 11 (1955): 422-61; part II: 12 (1956): 73-113; part III: 12 (1956) : 388-452; part IV: 13 (1957): 35-114, 394-481.

569
Richard of Pophis. *Zur Kenntnis der Formularsammlung des Richard von Pofi.* Ed. Ernst Batzer. Heidelberger Abhandlungen zur mittleren und neueren Geschichte 28. (Heidelberg, 1910).

570

Schmale, Franz-Josef. "Der Briefsteller Bernhards von Meung." *MIÖG* 66 (1958): 1-28.

571

Taylor, John. "Letters and Letter-collections in England, 1300-1420." *Nottingham Medieval Studies* 28 (1980): 57-70.

572

Voigts, Linda E. "Letter from a Middle English Dictaminal Formulary in Harvard Law Library MS 43." *Speculum* 56 (1981): 575-81.

573

Wieruszowski, Helene. "Twelfth-century 'Ars dictaminis' in the Barberini Collection of the Vatican Library." *Traditio* 18 (1962): 382-93.

> *This is a letter-collection, despite the title.*

574

Zeumer, Karolus, ed. *Marculfi formulae.* MGH, Legum, 5: Formulae. (Hanover, 1886). Pp. 32-106.

> *Marculf's* formulae *of the seventh century reveal an interesting use of pre-set forms for letters in which only the pertinent names and dates needed to be changed by a "writer." For a description of this and other early formulary collections see Giry.*

F. *Ars notaria*

575

Barraclough, Geoffrey. *Public Notaries and the Papal Curia: A Calendar and a Study of a Formularium Notariorum Curie from the Early Years of the Fourteenth Century.* (Rome, 1934).

576

Dibben, L.B. "Secretaries in the Thirteenth and Fourteenth Centuries." *EHR* 25 (1910): 430-44.

577
John of Tilbury. *Ars notaria*, ed. Valentin Rose in "*Ars notaria*: Tironische Noten und Stenographie im 12. Jahrhundert." *Hermes* 8 (1874): 303-26.
> *This is the text of an* Ars notaria *(c.1174) by the Englishman John of Tilbury. John includes a discussion of an elementary type of shorthand to be used in transcription.*

578
Kantorowicz, Hermann U., and W.W. Buckland, eds. *Studies in the Glossators of the Roman Law: Newly Discovered Writings of the Twelfth Century.* (Cambridge, England, 1938).

579
Lang, Albert. "Rhetorische Einflüsse auf die Behandlung des Prozesses in der Kanonistik des 12. Jahrhunderts." In *Festschrift Eduard Eichmann.* Ed. Martin Grabmann and Karl Hofmann. (Paderborn, 1940). Pp. 69-97.

580
Peter of Hallis. *Summa de literis missilibus: Ein Formelbuch aus Petri de Hallis.* Ed. Friedrich Firnhaber. Fontes rerum austriacarum, Österreichische Geschichts-Quellen, part II, vol. 6. (Vienna, 1853). Pp. 1-123.

581
[Pseudo-Irenius]. *Il "Formularium tabellionum" di Irnerio.* Ed. G.B. Palmieri. In *Appunti e documenti per la storia dei glossatori.* (Bologna, 1892).
> *Hermann Kantorowicz points out, p. 36, that this notarial text, attributed to Irenius (fl. 1118) by Palmieri, was written by an anonymous notary of Bologna about 1205.*

582
Rainerius of Perugia. *Ars notariae.* Ed. Ludwig Wahrmund. Quellen zur Geschichte des römisch-kanonischen Prozesses im Mittelalter 3, Heft 2. (Innsbruck, 1917).
> *Rainerius of Perugia's treatise, written 1226-33, demonstrates the close connection between law and the notarial profession.*

V
Poetics and Grammar:
Ars poetriae

During a period of about 75 years beginning in 1175, European grammar masters composed six Latin treatises giving direction to writers of verse and prose. The term *Arts of Poetry* is often applied collectively to these works, especially since the appearance of Faral's *Les arts poétiques* in 1924. Faral noted the influence of Ciceronian rhetoric in several of them, notably the *Poetria nova* of Geoffrey of Vinsauf. Later scholars like Manly and Atkins simply called these authors "rhetoricians."

The interest in their rhetorical aspects, however, has often obscured the fact that all these treatises were composed by practicing teachers of the *ars grammatica*. There is growing evidence that twelfth and thirteenth century grammar masters (and later ones, for that matter) employed sophisticated teaching methods refined from inherited Roman practices and adapted to a culture in which Latin was always a second or "foreign" language to students. These methods included the use of precept, imitation (both oral and written), progymnasmatic exercises, and continuing drill in language use. The aim was facility in both prose and verse forms. It no doubt seemed natural to these masters that all the available disciplines should be used for this purpose, regardless of whether certain ideas were "grammatical" or "rhetorical." Both Horace and Cicero were valuable. (And, as Hugh of St. Victor, John of Salisbury, and Alain de Lille point out in the twelfth century, "dialectic" could also be used to enhance language facility in students.)

Consequently any serious study of these *artes* must include an investigation into the grammatical as well as the rhetorical milieu of the time. Medieval grammarians went far beyond the simple syntactical concerns of Donatus and Priscian, seeking preceptive advice for the future writers and speakers who were their students. The commonly accepted division of discourse into "prosaic, metric, and rhythmic," after all, allowed ambitious grammarians ample scope to undertake study of all aspects of composition under any or all of those forms. By the thirteenth century grammarians are also found giving preceptive advice to letter-writers about style, and to preachers and hymn-writers about rhythmical patterns. Meanwhile at Oxford and Paris dialectically-inspired research into the nature of language by university masters led some grammarians into a concern for "modes of signification," resulting in the movement known as *Grammatica speculativa* (see Robins, Pinborg, Bursill-Hall, etc.).

Medieval grammar, including its teaching practices, is therefore an extremely complex subject which is only now being explored in depth. The "arts of poetry" are embedded in this cultural environment, however, and this is a factor to be kept in mind by any serious student.

It might be noted also that a number of vernacular arts of poetry appeared in the fourteenth and fifteenth centuries, works like the Provençal *Las Leys d'Amors* or the Castilian *El arte de trobar*. (These are to be described by Douglas Kelly in a forthcoming volume of the *Typology of Sources* series.)

A. History: Six Basic Studies

583

Brearley, Denis G. "Bibliography of Recent Publications Concerning the History of Grammar During the Carolingian Renaissance." *Studi Medievali* NS 3.21 (1980): 917-23.

584

Hunt, Richard W. *History of Grammar in the Middle Ages: Collected Papers.* Ed. Geoffrey L. Bursill-Hall. Amsterdam Studies in the Theory and History of Linguistic Science; Series III: Studies in the History of Linguistics, Vol. 5. (Amsterdam, 1980).

> *Seven previously-published essays by one of the greatest modern students of the history of medieval grammar. A useful bibliography (pp. xxvii-xxxvi) is added by the editor. Includes an Index of 173 technical terms. Indispensable for any student of the* Trivium.

585

Murphy, James J. "Ars poetriae: Preceptive Grammar, or The Rhetoric of Verse-Writing." In *Rhetoric in the Middle Ages.* Pp. 135-193.

586

Robins, Robert H. *Ancient and Medieval Grammatical Theory in Europe.* (London, 1951; rpt. New York, 1971).

> *This brief but important discussion of medieval grammatical theory, especially that of "speculative grammar," includes the best short treatment in English of the* modistae, *the authors of works on "modes of signification."*

587

Sivo, Vito. "Studi sui trattati grammaticali mediolatini." *Quaderni medievali* 11 (1981): 232-44.

> *Bibliographic survey of research on nineteen medieval grammatical writers, mainly prior to A.D. 1200.*

588

Thurot, Charles. "Notices et extraits de divers manuscrits latins pour servir à l'histoire des doctrines grammaticales au moyen âge." *Notices et extraits* 22 (1868): 1-592. (Reprinted Frankfurt-am-Main, 1964.)

> *This detailed work is absolutely indispensable to a study of any aspect of medieval grammar, poetics, or related subjects. It is arranged by centuries, with manuscript lists, excerpts of texts, author ascriptions, and discussion of significances of each item listed. After more than a century, it remains the only comprehensive attempt at outlining the whole field of medieval grammar. Thurot includes a useful index section covering proper names, incipits, and manuscripts. Readers may find especially illuminating his early chapters on medieval concepts of grammar, and on teaching methods in Italy as compared with those in northern Europe.*

B. General Studies

589
Allen, Judson B. "Hermann the German's Averroistic Aristotle and Medieval Poetic Theory." *Mosaic* 9 (1976): 67-81.

590
Bagni, Paolo. "Grammatica e Retorica nella Cultura Medievale." *Rhetorica* 2 (1984): 267-280.

591
Bagni, Paolo. *La costituzione della poesia nelle artes del XII-XIII secolo.* Università degli Studi di Bologna facoltà di lettere e filosofia: Studi e Ricerche, N.S. 20. (Bologna, 1968).

> *Treats the* artes *(pp. 57-126) and includes a section on "tematica emergente" (pp. 127-149).*

592
Baldwin, Charles S. "Cicero on Parnassus." *PMLA* 42 (1927): 106-12.

593
Bertini, F. "Letteratura latina medievale." Enciclopedia Europea XII: Bibliografia, Repertorio, Statistiche. (Milan, 1984).

> *Includes a section on rhetoric.*

594

Boggess, William F. "Aristotle's *Poetics* in the Fourteenth Century." *Studies in Philology* 67 (1970): 278-94.

595

Chenu, Marie-Dominique. "Grammaire et théologie aux XIIe et XIIIe siècles." *Archives d'histoire doctrinale et littéraire du moyen âge* 10 (1936): 5-28.

596

Dahan, Gilbert. "Notes et textes sur la poétique au moyen age." *AHDLM* 47 (1980): 171-239.

> *A brief survey of medieval philosophic views of poetry, especially in relation to* Aristotle's Poetics, *followed by four Latin texts (pp. 193-239) including the previously-unedited* Exposito supra Poetriam *(1307) of Barthélemy de Bruges from Paris B.N. Ms. Lat. 16809.*

597

Goldin, Claudia Dale, ed. *Retorica e poetica. Atti del III convegno italo-tedesco (Bressanone 1975).* Quaderni circolo filologico linguistico Padovano, 10. (Padua, 1979).

598

Guisberti, F., ed. "Twelfth Century Theological Grammar." In *Materials for a Study on Twelfth Century Scholasticism.* Ed. A. Maierù and G. Polara. History of Logic, 2. (Naples, 1982). Pp. 87-109.

> *The text studied is Peter's Chanter's* De Tropis Loquendi.

599

Haidu, P. "Repetition: Modern Reflections on Medieval Aesthetics." *Modern Language Notes* 92 (1977): 875-87.

600

Hunt, Richard W. "Introduction to the 'Artes' in the Twelfth Century." In *Studia mediaevalia in honorem admodum Reverendi Patris Raymundi Josephi Martin.* (Bruges, 1948). Pp. 85-112.

601

Hunt, R.W. *Schools and the Cloister: The Life and Writings of Alexander Nequam (1157-1217).* Ed. Margaret Gibson. (Oxford,

1984).
> *A posthumous editing of materials collected for many years by the late keeper of Western Manuscripts at the Bodleian Library, Oxford.*

602
Irvine, Martin. "Medieval Grammatical Theory and Chaucer's *House of Fame.*" *Speculum* 60 (1985): 850-876.
> *Argues that "Chaucer relies upon, and assumes his reader's acquaintance with some commonplaces of grammatica on the topics of speech, writing, texts, and history."*

603
Leclercq, Jean. "Le 'De grammatica' de Hugues de Saint-Victor." *Archives d'histoire doctrinale et littéraire du moyen âge* 14 (1945): 263-322.
> *Leclercq includes the text, pp. 268-322.*

604
Lutz, Eckard Conrad. *Rhetorica divina: Mittelhochdeutsches Prologgebete und die rhetorische kultur des Mittelalters.* Quellen und Forschungen zur Sprach- und Kulturgeschichte der germanischen Volker, neue folge, 82 (206). (Berlin, 1984).
> *A stimulating study whose scope is wider than the subtitle might indicate: the author compares the "opening prayer" of certain literary works with exordial theories of ancient rhetoric, the* ars dictandi, *the* ars poeticae, *and the* ars praedicandi. *The book's title derives from a passage in William of Auvergne's* Rhetorica divina.

605
Minnis, Alastair J. "Literary Theory in Discussions of *Formae tractandi* by Medieval Theologians." *New Literary History* 11 (1979-80): 133-45.
> *Discusses new forms "discovered" in biblical texts by theologians who believed that traditional rhetoric and poetics did not provide an adequate theoretical base for interpretation.*

606

Nims, Margaret F. "Ars poetica." In *A Dictionary of the Middle Ages*. Ed. Joseph R. Strayer. 13 vols. (New York, 1982-). Vol. I (1982), 553-555.

607

Olson, Glending. "Deschamps' *Art de dictier* and Chaucer's Literary Enviroment." *Speculum* 48 (1973): 714-723.

Regards Deschamps' work as natural music designed to delight rather than teach.

608

Payen, Jean-Charles. "Rhétorique ou poétique de l'imaginaire? Sur la fonction de l'allégorie à la fin du Moyen Age (à propos d'un livre récent)." *Studi francesi* 74 (1981): 280-5.

609

Scaglione, Aldo. "La teoria dello Stile Latino tra Medioevo e Umanesimo." In *Civiltà dell' Umanesimo*. Atti del VI, VII, VIII Convegno di studi umanistici. A cura di G. Tarugi. (Florence, 1972). Pp. 313-4.

610

Schultz, James A. "Classical Rhetoric, Medieval Poetics, and the Medieval Vernacular Prologue." *Speculum* 59 (1984): 1-15.

Argues that vernacular literature in France and Germany developed prologue traditions based on rhetorical theories.

611

Thiry, Claude. "Rhetorique et genres litteraires au XVe siècle." In *Sémantique lexicale et sémantique grammaticale en Moyen français: Colloque organisé par le Centre d'études Linguistiques et Litteraires de la Vrije Universiteit Brussel (28-29 Septembre, 1978)*. Ed. Marc Wilmet. (Brussels, 1980). Pp. 23-50.

612

Thomson, David. "Oxford Grammar Masters Revisited." *MS* 45 (1983): 298-310.

Discusses the teaching methods of fourteenth century grammar masters.

613
Trimpi, Wesley. "Quality of Fiction: The Rhetorical Transmission of Literary Theory." *Traditio* 30 (1974): 1-118.

614
Trevet, Nicholas. *Commento alle "Troades" di Seneca, Nicola Trevet.* Ed. M. Palma. (Roma, 1977).

615
Ziolkowski, Jan. "Avatars of Ugliness in Medieval Literature." *Modern Language Review* 79 (1984): 1-20.
Comments on the longevity of rhetorical patterns of descriptio *in literature, especially English literature.*

616
Zumthor, Paul. "Great Game of Rhetoric." *New Literary History* 12 (1980-81): 493-508.

617
Zumthor, Paul. *Langue, texte, énigme.* (Paris, 1975).
Includes an historical section.

C. Grammar in the Middle Ages

I. Basic Grammar and Syntax

618
Alexander of Villa Dei. *Das Doctrinale des Alexander de Villa-Dei.* Ed. Dietrich Reichling. In *Monumenta germaniae paedagogica 12.* (Berlin, 1893).
This hexameter rendering (1199) of the basic grammatical doctrine of Priscian rapidly became the standard advanced grammar text throughout Europe and was still being required in some universities in the seventeenth century. Reichling's introduction, pages cxix-cccix, includes a section on manuscripts and editions, listing some 239 extant manuscripts and 267 printed editions of the Doctrinale.

619

Alexander of Villa Dei. *Ecclesiale by Alexander of Villa Dei.* Ed. and trans. L.R. Lind. (Lawrence, Kansas, 1958).

While this Latin work of Alexander's may be of interest primarily to liturgists, Lind's brief introduction gives a capsule summary of the writer's career and influence.

620

Anonymous. *[Ars grammatica et rhetorica]: I trattati di grammatica e di retorica del cod. Casanatense 1086.* Ed. Camillo Morelli. (Rome, 1910).

This tenth-century piece is actually a commentary on Donatus and Priscian. Morelli prints only excerpts, not the complete text. Despite the title, the only "rhetoric" is in a discussion of figures that follows Donatus, though Cicero is mentioned.

621

Anselm. *De grammatico of St. Anselm.* Ed. Desmond P. Henry. (University of Notre Dame Press, 1964).

622

Ashworth, E.J. *Tradition of Medieval Logic and Speculative Grammar.* Subsidia medievalia, 9. (Toronto, 1978).

Bibliography of 880 items published between 1836 and 1976.

623

Bursill-Hall, Geoffrey L. "Medieval Donatus Commentaries." *Historiographia Linguistica* 8 (1981): 69-97.

624

Bursill-Hall, Geoffrey L. "Middle Ages." In *Historiography of Linguistics.* Ed. Thomas Seboek. Current Trends in Lingustics, 13. (The Hague, 1975).

Includes (pp. 190-196) the titles and incipits of 80 key grammatical texts.

625

Bursill-Hall, Geoffrey L. "Towards a History of Linguistics in the Middle Ages, 1100-1450." In *Studies in the History of Linguistics.* Ed. Dell Hymes. (Indiana University Press, 1974). Pp. 77-92.

626
Evrard of Béthune. *Eberhardi Bethuniensis Graecismus*. Ed. Ioh. Wrobel. Corpus grammaticorum medii aevi 1. (Wratislava, 1887).
> *This is a basic grammatical text which ranks with Alexander de Villa Dei's* Doctrinale *in popularity. It takes its name from the first word of a section discussing Greek terms.*

627
Gibson, Margaret. "Early Scholastic 'Glosule' to Priscian, 'Institutiones Grammaticae': The Text and its Influence." *Studi Medievali* NS 3:20 (1979): 235-54.
> *The text of the 'Glosule' appears on pp. 248-51.*

628
Gibson, Margaret T. "Priscian *Institutiones grammaticae*: A Hand-list of Manuscripts." *Scriptorium* 26 (1972): 105-24.
> *Lists 527 manuscripts.*

629
Gibson, Margaret T. and Tolson, J.E. "Summa of Petrus Helias on Priscianus minor." *CIMAGL* 27 (1978): 2-158.

630
Grosjean, Paul. "Quelques remarques sur Virgile le grammairien." In *Medieval Studies presented to Aubrey Gwynn, S.J..* Ed. J.A. Watt, J.B. Morall, F.X. Martin. (Dublin, 1961). Pp. 393-408.

631
[Henry of Avranches]. *Two Types of Thirteenth Century Grammatical Poems.* Ed. John P. Heironimus and Josiah C. Russell. Colorado College Publication, General Series 158, Language Series 111. 3. (Colorado Springs, 1929).
> *This is an edition of the* Libellus Donati metrice compositus *and of section II,* Equivoca, *of the* Comoda gramatice. *The pagination is faulty; pages 18-20 should follow 21-3.*

632
Huntsman, Jeffrey F. "Grammar." In *The Seven Liberal Arts in the Middle Ages.* Ed. David L. Wagner. (Indiana University

Press, 1983). Pp. 58-95.

Identifies three classical traditions underlying medieval grammar, as well as two "branches" (pedagogical and scholarly) of grammar in the middle ages. The excellent notes provide a valuable introduction to modern scholarship on the subject, and there is a useful chart (p. 65) outlining its development from ancient times to the Renaissance.

633

Hurlbut, Stephen A. "Forerunner of Alexander of Villa-dei." *Speculum* 8 (1933): 258-63.

634

Kelly, Louis G. *La grammaire à la fin du Moyen Age et les universaux. Essai de bibliographie.* (Lille, 1977).

635

Kneepkens, C.H., ed. " 'Ecce quod usus habet': Eine Quelle von Eberhard von Béthunes 'Grecismus,' Cap. V: 'De commutatione litterarum.' " *Mittellateinisches Jahrbuch* 16 (1981): 212-16.

636

Koerner, Konrad. "Medieval Linguistic Thought: A Comprehensive Bibliography." *Historiographia Linguistica* 7 (1980): 265-9.

637

Matonis, Ann T.E. "Welsh Bardic Grammars and the Western Grammatical Tradition." *Modern Philology* 79 (1981): 121-45.

Shows how medieval Welsh grammars derive from Latin sources and are pedagogic in purpose.

638

Scaglione, Aldo. *Ars grammatica: A Bibliographic Survey, Two Essays on the Grammar of the Latin and Italian Subjunctive, and A Note on the Ablative Absolute.* Janua Linguarum, Series Minor, 77. (The Hague, 1970).

Includes a valuable bibliographic survey indispensable to anyone wishing to begin work on medieval grammar and its relations to rhetoric and dialectic.

639
Schmücker, Laurentius, ed. *Robertus Kilwardby O.P.: In Donati artem maiorem III.* (Brixen/Bressanone, 1984).

640
Thomson, S. Harrison. "Robert Kilwardby's Commentaries *In Priscianum* and *In Barbarismum Donati.*" *NS* 12 (1938): 52-65.

II. Teaching of Grammar

641
Bernardus Silvestris. *Commentum Bernardi Silvestris super sex libros Eneidos Vergilii.* Ed. Guilielmus Riedel. (Greifswald, 1924).

642
Bursill-Hall, Geoffrey L. "Teaching Grammars of the Middle Ages: Notes on the Manuscript Tradition." *Historiographia Linguistica* 4 (1977): 1-29.

643
Clogan, Paul. "Literary Genres in a Medieval Textbook." *Medievalia et Humanistica* N.S. 11 (1982): 199-209.

> *The textbook is* Liber Catonianus *(13 mss.), which Clogan calls "a standard medieval school reader which was used in a curriculum of instruction in grammar in the thirteenth and fourteenth centuries." Six Latin authors appear in its final form: Cato, Theodolus, Avianus, Maximianus, Statius and Claudian.*

644
Faral, Edmond. "Le manuscrit 511 du 'Hunterian Museum' de Glasgow." *Studi medievali* NS 9 (1936): 18-119.

> *A major study of a teaching anthology (c. 1225). Faral notes that the 58 Latin poems in the manuscript form "une collection de traités de l'art d'écrire, accompagnés d'une anthologie soit de pièces de maîtres, soit de travaux d'ecoliers" (p. 117). The manuscript includes treatises of Matthew of Vendôme, Geoffrey of Vinsauf, and Gervais of Melkley. See Harbert.*

645

Guillaume of Conches. *Glosae in Juvenalem.* Ed. Bradford Wilson. Textes philosophiques du Moyen Âge, XVIII. (Paris, 1980).

646

Harbert, Bruce, ed. *Thirteenth-Century Anthology of Rhetorical Poems. Glasgow MS. Hunterian V.8.14.* Toronto Medieval Latin Texts, 4. (Toronto, 1975).

> *"A handbook of the rhetorical art" which contains treatises of Matthew of Vendôme, Geoffrey of Vinsauf, and Gervais of Melkley together with 49 poems on miscellaneous topics which illustrate precepts from the treatises. Harbert prints the poems only from this manuscript (formerly MS 511); the three major treatises are published by Faral.*

647

Henry, Desmond P. "Why 'Grammaticus'?" *Archivum latinitatis medii aevi (Bulletin du Cange)* 28 (1958): 165-80.

648

Hunt, Richard W. "Oxford Grammar Masters in the Middle Ages." *Oxford Studies Presented to Daniel Callus.* Oxford Historical Society NS 16. (Oxford, 1964).

649

Hunt, Richard W. "Studies on Priscian in the Eleventh and Twelfth Centuries, I: Petrus Helias and his Predecessors." *MARS* 1 (1941-3): 194-231.

650

Hunt, Richard W. "Studies on Priscian in the Twelfth Century, II: The School of Ralph of Beauvais." *MARS* 2 (1950): 1-56.

651

Leclercq, Jean. "Smaragde et la grammaire chrétienne." *Revue du moyen âge latin* 4 (1948): 15-22.

652

Marti, Berthe M. "Literary Criticism in the Mediaeval Commentaries on Lucan." *Transactions and Proceedings of the American Philological Association* 72 (1941): 245-54.

653
O'Donnell, J. Reginald. "Sources and Meaning of Bernard Silvester's Commentary on the *Aeneid*." *MS* 24 (1962): 233-49.

654
Rigg, A.G. "Medieval Latin Poetic Anthologies (IV)." *MS* 43 (1981): 472-97.
Includes references (472-473) to three preceding studies in the same journal.

655
Russell, Josiah C. "Alexander Neckam in England." In *Twelfth Century Studies*. (New York, 1978). Pp. 155-66.

656
Salmon, Paul. "Über den Beitrag des grammatischen Unterrichts zur Poetik des Mittelalters." *Archiv für das Studium der neuern Sprachen und Literaturen* 199 (1962): 65-84.

III. 'Speculative' Grammar *(De modis significandi)*

657
Bursill-Hall, Geoffrey L. *Speculative Grammars of the Middle Ages: The Doctrine of Partes orationis of the Modistae.* Approaches to Semiotics, 11. (The Hague, 1971).
Detailed analysis of modistic doctrines. Includes Glossary (pp. 392-99) of 41 key terms used by Martin of Dacia, Siger of Courtrai, and Thomas of Erfurt.

658
Gerson, Jean. *De modis significandi.* Ed. Walter Dress. In *Die Theologie Gersons.* (Gütersloh, 1931).

659
Grabmann, Martin. "Die geschichtliche Entwicklung der mittelalterlichen Sprachphilosophie und Sprachlogik: Ein Überblick." In *Mélanges Joseph de Ghellinck, S.J.* Museum Lessianum, Section Historique, 13-14. (Gembloux, Belgium, 1951). Vol. 2, 421-33.
This gives a good survey of early scholarship on the subject.

660

Grabmann, Martin. *Thomas von Erfurt und die Sprachlogik des mittelalterlichen Aristotelismus.* (Munich, 1943).

661

John of Dacia. *Summa gramatica.* In *Johannis Daci opera.* Ed. Alfredus Otto. Corpus philosophorum danicorum medii aevi, 2 parts, 1. (Copenhagen, 1955). Pp. 45-511 (text).

> *John's* Summa *(c.1280) was apparently written while he was teaching at Paris 1260-80 along with Martin of Dacia and at least two other Danes.*

662

Kelly, Louis G. "*De modis generandi*: Points of Contact between Noam Chomsky and Thomas of Erfurt." *Folia Linguistica* 5 (1971): 225-252.

663

Kelly, Louis G. "*Modus significandi*: An Interdisciplinary concept." *Historiographia Linguistica* 6 (1979): 159-80.

664

Martin of Dacia. *Modi Significandi.* In *Martin de Dacia opera.* Corpus philosophorum danicorum medii aevi 2. Ed. Henricus Roos. (Copenhagen, 1961). Pp. text 1-118.

665

Pinborg, Jan. *Die Entwicklung der Sprachtheorie im Mittelalter.* Beiträge zur Geschichte der Philosophie und Theologie des Mittelalters 42, Heft 2. (Münster, 1967).

> *An important account of scholastic grammar, including treatment of the opponents of the* modistae.

666

Pinborg, Jan. *Logik und Semantik im Mittelalter: Ein Überblick.* (Stuttgart, 1972).

667

Roos, Heinrich. *Die Modi significandi des Martinus de Dacia: Forschungen zur Geschichte der Sprachlogik im Mittelalter.* Beiträge zur Geschichte der Philosophie des Mittelalters 37, Heft 2. (Münster, [1952]).

668
Thomas of Erfurt. *Grammatica speculativa.* Ed. and trans. Geoffrey L. Bursill-Hall. (London, 1972).

> *An extremely useful volume which not only provides the text and translation of a central work in this area of grammatical study but also includes a concise study of medieval grammatical theory by the editor. Bursill-Hall describes this work as 'a complete statement of Modistic views on grammar.' Latin and English texts are on facing pages.*

669
"Tractatus de grammatica": Eine fälschlich Robert Grosseteste zu geschriebene spekulative Grammatik. Ed. and trans. Karl Reichl. Edition und Kommentar. Veröffentlichungen des Grabmann-Institutes, NF 28. (Munich, 1976).

> *Edition of a pre-modistic text, possibly written in mid-thirteenth-century Oxford by someone in the circle of Grosseteste.*

670
Van Steenberghen, Fernand. *Maître Siger de Brabant.* (Louvain, 1977).

D. *Ars poetriae* (*Ars metrica*)

I. Collections of Texts

671
Faral, Edmond. *Les arts poétiques du XIIe et du XIIIe siècle.* Bibliothèque de l'école des hautes études, fascicule 238. (Paris, 1924). (Reprinted Paris, 1958.)

> *The standard collection of texts of major* artes poetriae *with brief biographies, it contains texts, among others, of the following: Matthew of Vendome,* Ars versificatoria *; Geoffrey of Vinsauf,* Poetria nova; *Geoffrey of Vinsauf,* Documentum de

modo et arte dictandi et versificandi *(prose version of* Poetria nova*); Geoffrey of Vinsauf,* De coloribus rhetoricis*; Eberhard the German,* Laborintus*. Faral also gives summaries of Gervais of Melkley,* Ars versificaria*, and John of Garland,* Poetria [De arte prosayca metrica et rithmica]. *Part two (pp. 55-103) provides an analysis of the basic doctrines of the* artes poetriae*, while a brief chapter on tropes and figures (pp. 48-54) traces the influence of the pseudo-Ciceronian* Rhetorica ad Herennium *on six of these* artes.

672

Leyser, Polycarp. *Historia poetarum et poematum medii aevi.* (Magdeburg, 1721).

This collection of Latin texts of artes poetriae *is now largely supplanted by Faral,* Les arts poétiques.

673

Sedgwick, Walter B. "Style and Vocabulary of the Latin Arts of Poetry of the Twelfth and Thirteenth Centuries." *Speculum* 3 (1928): 349-81.

The article is a supplement to Faral's Les arts poétiques *and includes a word index to Faral's collection as well as summaries of the chief* artes poetriae.

II. General Studies

674

Atkins, John W.H. *English Literary Criticism: The Medieval Phase.* (Cambridge University Press, 1943). (Reprinted London, 1952.)

Atkin's work is very uneven, although it contains much useful analysis of the artes poetriae *in particular. Its critical judgements should be regarded with caution.*

675

Bagni, Paolo. "L'*Inventio* nell'Ars Poetica Latino-Medievale." In *Rhetoric Revalued: Papers from the International Society for the History of Rhetoric.* Ed. Brian Vickers. (Binghamton, New York,

1982). Pp. 99-114.

676
Johannes de Hanvilla. *Architrenius.* Ed. P.G. Schmidt. (Munich, 1974).

> *This allegorical satire by Jean de Hanville (twelfth century) is a frequent source for writers of the* ars poetriae, *and is cited into the fifteenth century.*

677
Kelly, Douglas. *Medieval Imagination: Rhetoric and the Poetry of Courtly Love.* (University of Wisconsin Press, 1978).

678
Klopsch, Paul. *Einführung in die Dichtungslehren des lateinischen Mittelalters.* (Darmstadt, 1980).

> *Includes discussions of the theories of Matthew of Vendome, Geoffrey of Vinsauf, and John of Garland, as well as a critique of the views of Ernst Curtius.*

679
Knapp, Fritz P. "Vergleich und Exempel in der lateinischen Rhetorik und Poetik von der Mitte des 12. bis zur Mitte des 13. Jahrhunderts." *Studi Medievali* NS 3.14 (1973): 443-511.

680
Ogle, Marbury B. "Some Aspects of Mediaeval Latin Style." *Speculum* 1 (1926): 170-89.

> *One of the earliest studies to suggest that rhetorical teachings might underlie observable differences in the style of medieval authors.*

681
Patterson, Warner F. *Three Centuries of French Poetic Theory: A Critical History of the Chief Arts of Poetry in France (1328-1630).* University of Michigan Publications in Language and Literature 14-15. (1935).

682
Quadlbauer, Franz. *Die antike Theorie der Genera dicendi im lateinischen Mittelalter.* Österreichische Akademie der Wissenschaften, Philosophisch-Historische Klasse, Sitzungsberichte 241,

Band 2. (Vienna, 1962).

> The author criticizes the thesis of Faral that levels of diction in the middle ages were determined primarily by the social level of the people involved.

683

Quadlbauer, Franz. "Zu Theorie der Komposition in der mittelalterlichen Rhetorik und Poetik." In *Rhetoric Revalued: Papers from the International Society for the History of Rhetoric.* Ed. Brian Vickers. (Binghamton, New York, 1982). Pp. 115-31.

III. Authors and Works

Eberhard

684

Carlson, Evelyn, trans. "*Laborintus* of Eberhard rendered into English with Introduction and Notes." Unpublished MA thesis, Cornell University, 1930.

Geoffrey of Vinsauf: A. Works

685

Gallo, Ernest A. *Poetria Nova and Its Sources in Early Rhetorical Doctrine.* (The Hague, 1971).

> Translation of the Poetria nova based on the text of Faral, with Latin text on facing pages.

686

Kopp, Jane Baltzell. *Geoffrey of Vinsauf: The New Poetics.* In *Three Medieval Rhetorical Arts.* Ed. James J. Murphy. (University of California Press, 1971). Pp. 29-108.

> Translation of the Poetria nova from the text of Faral.

687

Nims, Margaret F., trans. *Poetria nova.* (Toronto, 1967).

> This is a good translation of Vinsauf's influential hexameter

work (1200-2). Since the introduction to the translation does not sufficiently explain its importance, however, the reader should also consult Atkins, Faral, Manly, and Murphy. For other translations see Gallo and Murphy, Three Arts.

688

Parr, Roger P., trans. *Documentum de modo et arte dictandi et versificandi (Instruction in the Method and Art of Speaking and Versifying).* (Marquette University Press, 1968).

While Parr's translation is adequate, his introduction is uneven and does not always include recent scholarship on key points. Geoffrey's prose Documentum *presents substantially the same doctrines as his hexameter* Poetria nova.

689

Woods, Marjorie Curry, ed. and trans. *Early Commentary on the 'Poetria nova' of Geoffrey of Vinsauf.* (New York, 1985).

Edition and translation, with extensive notes, of an anonymous commentary written "within a generation" of the Poetria nova. *This* In principio huius libri *commentary (so named from its incipit) is labelled by the editor as "type A" to distinguish it from other commentaries with similar beginnings. It was one of the most popular, surviving in eight manuscripts. The editor's notes and apparatus provide an excellent introduction to the Vinsaufian tradition.*

Geoffrey of Vinsauf: B. Secondary References

690

Commedie latine del XII e XIII secolo. Pubblicazioni dell'Istituto di filologia classica e medioevale, 48, 61. 2 vols. (Genoa: Università degli Studi, 1976 and 1980).

The second volume includes an edition of a Latin play, De tribus sociis, *attributed to Geoffrey of Vinsauf.*

691

Crespo, Roberto. "Brunetto Latini e la 'Poetria nova' di Geoffroi de Vinsauf." *Lettere Italiane* 24 (1972): 97-9.

692

Gallo, Ernest. "Grammarian's Rhetoric: The *Poetria nova* of Geoffrey of Vinsauf." In *Medieval Eloquence.* Pp. 68-84.

693

Licitra, Vincenzo. "La 'Summa de arte dictandi' di Maestro Goffredo." *Studi medievali* Series 3, 7 (1966): 865-913.

> *Includes text (pp. 885-913) of a* Summa *by "Gaufredus Bononiensis." Discusses earlier claims that the author of the* Summa *is Geoffrey of Vinsauf.*

694

Richardson, Janette. *Blameth Nat Me: A Study of Imagery in Chaucer's Fabliaux.* Studies in English Literature, 58. (The Hague, Paris, 1970).

> *Examines Chaucer's artistic debt to the academic rhetoricians—the representative rhetorical work being the* Poetria Nova *of Geoffrey of Vinsauf.*

Gervais of Melkley

695

Gervais von Melkley Ars poetica. Kritische ausgabe von Hans-Jürgen Gräbener. Forschungen zur romanischen Philologie, 17. (Münster Westfalen, 1965).

> *Edition of the* Ars versificaria *or* Ars poetica *(c. 1213-1216) of Gervasius de Saltu Lacteo (c. 1185-c. 1241).*

696

Giles, Catherine Yodice. "Gervais of Melkley's Treatise on the Art of Versifying and the Method of Composing in Prose." Ph.D diss. Rutgers University, 1973.

> *Includes a translation based on the Gräbener text.*

Guilhelm Molinier

697

Anglade, Joseph, ed. *Las leys d'amors.* 4 vols. (Toulouse, 1919-20).

This work, compiled by Guilhelm Molinier, chancellor of the Consistoire du Gai Savoir at Toulouse, was issued in 1356 as a comprehensive treatment of grammar, metrics, and rhetoric. Two prose versions and one in verse survive.

John of Garland: A. Works

698

Habel, Edwin, ed. "Die *Exempla honestae vitae* des Johannes de Garlandia, eine lateinische Poetik des 13. Jahrhunderts." *Romanische Forschungen* 29 (1911): 131-54.

The text appears on pp. 137-154.

699

Lawler, Traugott, ed. and trans. *Parisiana Poetria of John of Garland.* (Yale University Press, 1974).

Text and translation of Garland's De arte prosayce, metrica, et rithmica, *with excellent notes. Includes a brief excursus (pp. 327-328) on its relation to Vinsauf's* Documentum. *Garland's* De arte *is an ambitious attempt to gather into one work the basic lore of all three kinds of writing as understood by medieval theorists. The work does not take up each type separately, but instead strives to provide a unified approach to all the types.*

700

Mari, Giovanni, ed. "L'Arte' de Giovanni di Garlandi." In *I trattati medievali di ritmica latina.* Item v. Memorie del reale istituto lombardo di scienze e lettere 20. (Milan, 1899). Pp. 35-80.

The text is edited by Mari in two sections, of which this is one and the following item is the other. For translation see Lawler.

701

Mari, Giovanni, ed. "Poetria magistri Johannis anglici de arte prosayca metrica et rithmica." *Romanische Forschungen* 13 (1902): 883-965.

702

Paetow, Louis J., ed. *Morale scolarium of John of Garland*. Part II of *Two Medieval Satires on the University of Paris*, Memoirs of the University of California 4, part II. (Berkeley, 1927).

> *The introduction contains a useful summary of Garland's career and the sixty works attributed to him. See Henry of Andeli.*

John of Garland: B. Secondary References

703

Bursill-Hall, Geoffrey L. "Johannes de Garlandia: Forgotten Grammarian and the Manuscript Tradition." *Historiographia Linguistica* 3 (1976): 155-77.

704

Colker, Marvin L. "New Evidence that John of Garland Revised the *Doctrinale* of Alexander de Villa Dei." *Scriptorium* 28 (1974): 68-71.

705

Lawler, Traugott F. "John of Garland and Horace: A Medieval Schoolman faces the *Ars poetica*." *Classical Folia* 22 (1968): 3-13.

706

Speroni, Gian Battista. "Proposte per il testo della 'Parisiana Poetria' di Giovanni di Garlandia." *Studi medievali* NS 3. 20 (1979): 585-624.

707

Vecchi, Giuseppe. "Modi d'arte poetica in Giovanni di Garlandia e il ritmo *Aula vernat virginalis*." *Quadrivium* 1 (1956): 256-68.

> *Vecchi sees a connection between John of Garland's theory of allegory and the grammatical doctrine of wordchange,* transumptio.

708
Worstbrock, Franz Josef. "Johannes von Garlandia." In *Verfasserlexikon des Mittelalters*. (1983). Band 4, cols. 612-623.

Matthew of Vendôme: A. Works

709
Ars versificatoria (The Art of the Versemaker). Trans. and intro. Roger P. Parr. Medieval Philosophical Texts in Translation, No. 22. (Marquette University Press, 1981).
> *A competent if sometimes over-literal translation. The brief Introduction (13 pp.) makes no note of the other two earlier translations, and in fact the citations date generally to the 1960's and earlier.*

710
Mathei Vindocinensis Opera: I: Catalogo dei manoscritti. Ed. F. Munari. Vol. 144. Storia e letteratura, Raccolta di Studi e Testi. (Rome, 1977).
> *This first of three planned volumes provides descriptions of 126 manuscripts.*

711
Gallo, Ernest. "Matthew of Vendôme: Introductory Treatise on the Art of Poetry." *Proceedings of the American Philosophical Society*. 118 (1974): 51-93.
> *Includes translation (pp. 61-93).*

712
Galyon, Aubrey E. *Matthew of Vendôme: The Art of Versification*. (Iowa State Univ. Press, 1980).
> *A clear translation with brief introduction.*

713
Munari, F. "Matteo di Vendôme, 'Ars' 1.111." *Studi Medievali* NS 3. 17 (1976): 293-305.
> *Provisional edition of a section of Book One of the* Ars versificatoria.

714

Perugi, Maurizio. "Saggio di un'edizione critica dell' 'Ars versificatoria' di Matteo di Vendôme." In *Testi e interpretazioni: studi del Seminario di Filologia Romanza dell' Università di Firenze*. (Milan, 1978). Pp. 669-719.

> *Includes a provisional edition of the Prologue and paragraphs 1-11 of the second section, with a discussion of the* ars poetriae *in the twelfth century. [It might be noted that all three English translations of the* Ars versificatoria *are based on the 1924 text of Faral.]*

Nicolaus Dybinus

715

Jaffe, Samuel P. *Nicolaus Dybinus' 'Declaracio oracionis de beata Dorothea': Studies and Documents in the History of Late Medieval Rhetoric*. Beiträge zur Literatur des XV bis XVIII Jahrhunderts, 5. (Wiesbaden, 1974).

> *Editions of two of Dybinus' nine works: his* Oracio de beata Dorothea, *then two versions of the text of the commentary on that poem,* Declaracio oracionis de beata Dorothea. *Dybinus also wrote a commentary on Vinsauf's* Poetria nova *as well as a* Sertum rethorice, *a* Liber de ricmis, *and a* De modo tractandi tractatulus. *Jaffe notes that Dybinus'* Declaracio *was taught at the University of Vienna around the middle of the fifteenth century.*

716

Szklenar, Hans. *Magister Nicolaus de Dybin: Vorstudien zu einer Edition seiner Schriften: Ein Beitrag zur Geschichte der literarischen Rhetorik im späteren Mittelalter*. (Munich, 1981).

> *An excellent study of Dybin's works on rhetoric and his commentary on the* Laborintus *of Eberhardus Allemanus. Includes studies of manuscript relations. See also Jaffe.*

717

Szklenar, Hans. "Magister Nicolaus de Dybin als Lehrer des Rhetorik." *Daphnis: Zeitschrift für Mittlere Deutsche Literatur* XVI (1987): 1-12.

IV. Related Works

718

Boccaccio. *Boccaccio on Poetry: Being the Preface and the Fourteenth and Fifteenth Books of Boccaccio's Genealogia Deorum Gentilium.* Trans. Charles G. Osgood. (New York, 1956).

> Boccaccio defines poetry (p.39) as "a sort of fervid and exquisite invention, with fervid expression, in speech or writing, of that which the mind has invented."

719

Dante Alighieri. *Translation of the Latin Works of Dante Alighieri.* Trans. A.G. Ferrers Howell and Philip H. Wicksteed. (London, 1940).

> The translation of De vulgari eloquentia *appearing on pp. 1-124 is a revision of the version by Howell first published in 1890.*

720

Deschamps, Eustache. *L'Art de dictier.* In *Oeuvres complètes de Eustache Deschamps.* Ed. Marquis de Queux de Saint-Hilaire and Gaston Raynaud. Société des anciens textes français 7. (Paris, 1891). Pp. 266-92.

> Deschamp's work (1392) reflects the state of rhetorical influence on French poetic theory at that time.

E. The Art of Rhythmical Composition *(Ars rithmica)*

721

Janson, Tore. *Prose Rhythm in Medieval Latin from the 9th to the 13th Century.* Acta Universitatis Stockholmiensis, Studia Latina Stockholmiensia, XX. (1975).

> Proposes an analytic method of identifying prose patterns. Studies, among others, Peter of Blois, and concludes he could not have been author of the Libellus de arte dictandi rethorice (c. 1181). There is a detailed statistical analysis by Giovanni Orlandi in his review in Studi Medievali ser. 3.19.2 (1978),

701-18.

722

Mari, Giovanni, ed. *I trattati medievali di ritmica latina.* Memorie del reale istituto lombardo di scienze e lettere 20. (Milan, 1899). (Reprinted Bologna, 1971.)

This key collection of texts includes works by eight authors on the subject of ars rithmica. This remains a largely unexplored field despite the attention paid to the rhythmical prose style (cursus) of the ars dictaminis.

723

Vecchi, Giuseppe. "Sulla teoria dei ritmi mediolatini: problemi di classificazione." *Studi mediolatini e volgari* 8 (1960): 301-24.

F. Tropes and Figures

724

Alford, John A. "Grammatical Metaphor: A Survey of Its Use in the Middle Ages." *Speculum* 57 (1982): 728-760.

725

Arbusow, Leonid. *Colores rhetorici: Eine Auswahl rhetorischer Figuren und Gemeinplätze als Hilfsmittel für akademische Übungen an mittelalterlichen Texten.* (Göttingen, 1948).

Arbusow attempts to provide a systematic analysis of Latin colores but his book is poorly organized. See the review by Luitpold Wallach in Speculum 24(1949), 416-18. Compare Lausberg.

726

Conley, Thomas. "Byzantine Teaching on Figures and Tropes: An Introduction." *Rhetorica* 4 (1986): 335-374.

Includes tables (pp 368-374) comparing Greek figures and tropes treated by twelve authors.

727

Crawford, Samuel J., ed. and trans. *Byrhtferth's Manual.* Vol. 1 (all published). Early English Text Society 177. (Oxford

University Press, 1929).
> *This contains the first* OE *translation (1011) of the section on figures of speech* (schemata) *from Bede's* De schematibus et tropis.

728
Jacob, Ernest F. "*Florida verborum venustas*: Some Early Examples of Euphuism in England." *Bulletin of the John Rylands Library* 17 (1933): 264-90.

729
Johannes Balbus de Janua ["John of Genoa"]. *Catholicon*. (Mainz, 1460).
> *This thirteenth-century work is an extensive treatment of tropes, figures, and metaplasms; this edition is one of the earliest printed books and is attributed, with a query, to the press of Gutenburg. The work was frequently reprinted and there are 23 known editions to 1500. For finding lists see* Gesamtkatalog der Wiegendrucke 3 (Leipzig, 1928), 3182-205 *and* Incunabula in American Libraries, *compiled and ed. Frederick Goff (New York, 1964), B-20 through B-34.*

730
Kelly, Henry Ansgar. "*Occupatio* as Negative Narration: A Mistake for *Occultatio/Praeteritio*." *Modern Philology* 74 (1977): 311-15.

731
Krewitt, Ulrich. *Metaphor und Tropischen Rede in der Auffassung des Mittelalters*. Mittellateinisches Jahrbuch, Beiheft 7. (Rätingen, 1971).

732
Lausberg, Heinrich. *Handbuch der literarischen Rhetorik*. 2 vols. (Munich, 1960).
> *This is a useful catalogue of surviving ancient rhetorical concepts—especially figures and tropes—but it covers a period only up to* AD 600. *Compare Arbusow.*

733

Marbodus. *De ornamentis verborum.* In *PL* 171, cols. 1687-92.
This was a frequently copied set of figures.

734

Meyer, Paul. "Notice sur les *Corregationes Promethei* d'Alexandre Neckam." *Notices et extraits* 35 (1897): 641-82.
Despite Neckham's title, his work (1210) is a treatise on style, especially tropes and figures; Meyer prints the text of Alexander's Prologue. See also Pseudo-Cicero, Faral, and Onulf.

735

Nims, Margaret F. "Translatio: 'Difficult Statement' in Medieval Poetic Theory." *University of Toronto Quarterly* 43 (1974): 215-30.

G. Theory and Practice

736

Badel, Pierre-Yves. "La rhétorique et les grands rhétoriqueurs." *Réforme, Humanisme, Renaissance* 18 (1984): 3-11.

737

Baltzell, Jane. "Rhetorical 'Amplification' and 'Abbreviation' and the Structure of Medieval Narrative." *Pacific Coast Philology* 2 (1967): 32-9.

738

Beale, Walter H. "Rhetoric in the Old English Verse-paragraph." *Neuphilologische Mitteilungen* 80 (1979): 133-42.

739

Frey, Leonhard H. "Rhetoric of Latin Christian Epic Poetry." *Annuale medievale* 2 (1961): 15-30.

740

Hunt, Tony. "Aristotle, Dialectic, and Courtly Literature." *Viator* 10 (1979): 95-129.

741
James, Laurence. "L'"objet poétique' des Grands Rhétoriqueurs."
Annales de la Faculté des Lettres et Sciences Humaines de Nice 48
(1948): 225-234.
> *Discusses Eustace Deschamps, Pierre Fabri, Baudet Hérenc,*
> *and Jean Molinet. Includes a bibliography.*

742
Kliman, Bernice W. "John Barbour and Rhetorical Tradition."
Annuale Medievale 18 (1977): 106-35.

743
Langlois, Ernest. *Recueil d'arts de seconde rhétorique.* (Paris,
1902).
> *Langlois points out that the "second" rhetoric was concerned*
> *with verse, while the "first" was concerned with prose.*

744
Manly, John M. "Chaucer and the Rhetoricians." *PBA* 12 (1926):
95-113.
> *This study of the influence of Geoffrey of Vinsauf on Chaucer*
> *also makes some sweeping judgements on the former's general*
> *influence. See Murphy.*

745
Matonis, Ann. "Rhetorical Patterns in *Marwnad Llywelyn ap*
Gruffudd by Gruffudd ab yr Ynad Coch." *Studia Celtica* 14-15
(1979-80): 188-92.

746
McPherson, Clair Wade. The Influence of Latin Rhetoric on Old
English Poetry. Diss., English. (University of Washington Press,
1980).
> *"Latin rhetoric, given the system of monastic education and*
> *the consistency of interpretation provided by rhetorical*
> *interpretation, must be admitted as a major influence on Old*
> *English Poetry." (DAI 41A.3, 1980, p. 1065).*

747
Murphy, James J. "New Look at Chaucer and the Rhetoricians."
Review of English Studies NS 15 (1964): 1-20.

A critique of Manly's study on the influence of Geoffrey of Vinsauf on Chaucer. The article argues that regular grammatical training could have supplied Chaucer with his knowledge of tropes and figures.

748

Olsson, Kurt O. "Rhetoric, John Gower, and the Late Medieval *Exemplum.*" *Medievalia et Humanistica* N.S. 8 (1977): 185-200.

749

Pastré, Jean-Marc. *Rhétorique et adaptation dans les oeuvres allemandes du moyen-âge.* Publications de l'Université de Rouen, 50. (Paris: Presses Universitaires de France, 1979).

750

Patterson, Linda M. *Troubadors and Eloquence.* (Oxford: Clarendon Press, 1975).

751

Scaglione, Aldo. "Rhetoric in Italian Literature: Dante and the Rhetorical Theory of Sentence Structure." In *Medieval Eloquence.* Pp. 252-69.

752

Shapiro, Marianne. "Figurality in the *Vita Nuova*: Dante's New Rhetoric." *Dante Studies* 97 (1979): 107-27.

753

Turlin, Louis. "Notes sur Jean Robertet, grand rhétoriquer, sécretaire de Jean II de Bourbon." *Bulletin de la Société d'emulation du Bourbonnais. Lettres, sciences et arts* 59 (1979): 231-49.

754

Vance, Eugène. "Désir, rhétorique et texte. Semences de différence: Brunet Latin chez Dante." *Poétique* 42 (1980): 137-55.

755

Wiley, W.L. "Who named them Rhétoriqueurs?" In *Mediaeval Studies in Honor of Jeremiah Denis Matthias.* (Cambridge, Massachusetts, 1948).

756
Wolf, Rudolph H. *Der Stil der Rhétoriqueurs: Grundlagen und Grundformen*. (Giessen, 1939).

757
Zumthor, Paul. "From Hi(story) to Poem, or the Paths of Pun: the Grands Rhétoriqueurs of Fifteenth-Century France." *New Literary History* 10 (1979): 231-63.

758
Zumthor, Paul. "Le Carrefour des rhétoriquers: Intertextualité et rhétoriques." *Poétique* 27 (1976): 317-37.

VI

Sermon Theory:
Ars praedicandi

Medieval preaching, since it involved the oral communication of ideas from speaker to audience, might well have been expected to follow closely the precepts inherited from the ancient rhetoric designed to prepare Greek and Roman orators to speak to their audiences. However, this is not what happened. Ciceronian rhetoric was not simply applied to preaching, though Saint Augustine had recommended it.

Instead, around the year 1200 medieval preachers developed a different sermon pattern based on division and amplification of a Scriptural quotation (or "theme"). This "thematic" sermon differs in several important respects from the ancient *oratio* of Cicero, notably in that it provides for numerous points of amplification or "proof" rather than setting up a sequence of ideas leading to a conceptual conclusion. The earliest advocate of this new mode seems to have been Thomas Chabham (Thomas of

Salisbury), whose *De arte praedicandi* was written in England about 1205; this text is still unpublished, but is now being edited by a German scholar. The fact that more than 300 surviving preaching manuals follow essentially Chabham's model would seem to indicate that he was probably the founder or least an early advocate of this preaching genre.

Prior to Chabham only the most general advice for preachers is seen in the eight centuries following Augustine's defense of rhetoric in his *De doctrina Christiana* (426). Examples may be seen in the eleventh-century work of Guibert of Nogent and the twelfth-century treatise of Alain de Lille. The numerous scholastic commentaries on Cicero's rhetoric from the eleventh and twelfth centuries seem to have had little effect on preaching theory; rather, Chabham's treatise is eclectic, based on grammar, philosophy, literature, and logic as well as Roman rhetoric.

Until all the manuscript materials have been examined in greater detail it may not be possible to make a definitive assessment of the comparative influences of Ciceronian rhetoric, scholastic method, pastoral practice, and medieval grammar. The genre of the "thematic" sermon is so well-defined, however, that the modern reader can learn a great deal about it from reading Robert of Basevorn's *Forma praedicandi* (1322) as a "typical" manual.

A. History: Nine Basic Studies

759

Caplan, Harry. "Classical Rhetoric and the Mediaeval Theory of Preaching." *Classical Philology* 28 (1933): 73-96.

> *This is a fundamental study, arguing the influence of ancient rhetoric on medieval preaching theory.*

760

Dargan, Edwin C. *History of Preaching.* 2 vols. (New York, 1905). (Reprinted in one volume, 1954.)

This over-long book is an uncritical but still valuable survey of preachers, movements, and theological implications.

761

Davy, Marie Magdeleine. *Les Sermons universitaires parisiens de 1230-1231: contribution à l'histoire de la prédication médiévale.* Etudes de philosophie médiévale. Ed. Etienne Gilson. (Paris, 1931).

This work is important for a study of the origins of the "university-style" or "thematic" sermon; Davy prints the texts of a large number of Latin sermons delivered at Paris during the school year 1230-31.

762

Gilson, Etienne. "Michel Menot et la technique du sermon médiéval." In *Les Idées et les lettres.* (Paris, 1932). Pp. 93-154. (Reprinted from *Revue d'histoire franciscaine* 2 [1925], 301-50.)

Gilson's is one of the most important brief discussions of medieval preaching theory.

763

Longère, Jean. *La prédication médiévale.* (Paris, 1983).

A major, wide-ranging study dealing with a broad survey of subjects including sermon structure, vernacular preaching, preaching aids, and problems of scholarship in analyzing medieval sermons.

764

Murphy, James J. "*Ars praedicandi*: The Art of Preaching." In *Rhetoric in the Middle Ages.* Pp. 269-355.

Discusses the history of Judaic and Christian ideas about preaching, with special attention to the so-called "thematic" style of sermon developed by the beginning of the thirteenth century; includes a lengthy summary of a typical ars praedicandi *(the* Forma praedicandi *of Robert of Basevorn).*

765
Owst, Gerald R. *Preaching in Medieval England: An Introduction to Sermon Manuscripts of the Period, c. 1350-1450.* (Cambridge University Press, 1926). (Reprinted New York, 1965.)

Long a standard, this marvellously detailed study provides numerous insights into the everyday practices of medieval preachers. Chapters 8-9 (pp. 279-354) deal specifically with theoretical manuals and the sermon-making process.

766
Roth, Dorothea. *Die mittelalterliche Predigttheorie und das Manuale curatorum des Johann Ulrich Surgant.* Basler Beiträge zur Geschichtswissenschaft, 58. (Basel, 1956).

This important survey of sermon theory from Augustine to the fifteenth century is one of the most comprehensive treatments of authors, their works, and their relations to each other. Roth regards William of Auvergne's Rhetorica divina *(thirteenth century) as a turning point in the evolution of a truly medieval approach to preaching. Since the book is rare, readers may wish to consult the review by Gordon Leff in* JEH *8 (1957), 242-3.*

767
Smyth, Charles. *Art of Preaching: A Practical Survey of Preaching in the Church of England, 1747-1939.* Society for Promoting Christian Knowledge. (London, [1940]).

A brief but important survey of medieval theory is included. Smyth presents one of the most sensible short treatments of the subject available, and his book is useful for an introduction to the field.

B. General Studies

768

Anastasi, R. "Sulla funzione della retorica nell'omiletica cristiana e in Michele Psello." *Koinonia* 7 (1983): 57-59.

769

Bataillon, Louis-Jacques. "Approaches to the Study of Medieval Sermons." *Leeds Studies in English NS* 11 (1980): 19-35.

770

Berlioz, Jacques. "La memoire du prédicateur: recherche sur la memorisation des récits exemplaires (XIIIe-XVe siècles)." In *Temps, memoire, tradition au Moyen Age.* (Université de Provence, 1983). Pp. 157-183.

771

Berlioz, Jacques. "Le récit efficace: l'example au service de la prédication (XIIIe-XVe siècles)." *Mélanges de l'École française de Rome. Moyen Âge-temps modernes* 92 (1980): 113-46.

772

Bonmann, Ottokar. "Zur Geschichte der Homiletik im Mittelalter." *Franziskanische Studien* 25 (1938): 274-84.

773

Bourgain, Louis. *La Chaire française au XIIe siècle.* (Paris, 1879).

774

Brilioth, Ingve. *Brief History of Preaching.* Trans. Karl E. Mattson. (Philadelphia, [1965]).

775

Briscoe, Marianne G. "Ars praedicandi." In *A Dictionary of the Middle Ages.* Ed. Joseph R. Strayer. 13 vols. (New York, 1982-). Vol. I (1982), 555-558.

776

Bynum, Caroline Walker. *Docere verbo et exemplo: An Aspect of Twelfth-Century Spirituality.* Harvard Theological Studies, 31. (Missoula, Montana, 1979).

> *Argues that a reform movement toward a more active monastic life included emphasis on the importance of preaching.*

777
Callebaut, A. "Le Sermon historique d'Etudes de Châteauroux à Paris, le 18 mars, 1229: Autour de l'origine de la grève universitaire et de l'enseignement des mendiants." *Archivum franciscanum historicum* 28 (1935): 81-114.

778
Caplan, Harry. "Four Senses of Scriptural Interpretation and the Mediaeval Theory of Preaching." *Speculum* 4 (1929): 282-90.
   Caplan presents a clear description of the four "senses": literal, anagogical, tropological, and allegorical.

779
Caplan, Harry. "Rhetorical Invention in Some Mediaeval Tractates on Preaching." *Speculum* 2 (1927): 284-95.

780
Cespedes, Frank V. "Chaucer's Pardoner and Preaching." *Journal of English Literary History* 44 (1977): 1-18.

781
Cruel, Rudolf. *Geschichte der deutschen Predigt im Mittelalter.* (Detmold, 1879).

782
Dagens, Claude. "Gregoire le Grande et le ministère de la parole (Les notions d'"ordo praedicatorum' et d'"officium praedicationis')." In *Forma futuri: Studi in onore del Cardinale Michele Pellegrino.* (Turin, 1975). Pp. 1054-73.

783
D'Avray, David L. *Preaching of the Friars: Sermons Diffused from Paris before 1300.* (Oxford, 1985).
   Discusses the uses made of model sermon collections distributed from Paris, with implications for the actual value of formal artes praedicandi *in the production of sermons.*

784
Davy, Marie Magdeleine. "Les 'auctoritates' et les procédés de citation dans la prédication médiévale." *Revue d'histoire franciscaine* 8 (1931): 344-54.

785

Delcorno, Carlo. "'Ars praedicandi' e 'ars memorativa' nell'esperienza di San Bernardo da Siena." *Bulletino abruzzese di storia patria* 70 (1978).

786

Delcorno, Carlo. *Giordano da Pisa e l'antica predicazione volgare.* Biblioteca di "Lettere Italiane," 4. (Florence, 1975).

787

Delcorno, Carlo. "Origini della predicazione francescana." In *Francesco d'Assisi e francescanesimo dal 1216 al 1226. Atti del IV Convegno Internacionale, Assisi 1976.* (Assisi, 1977). Pp. 127-160.

788

Delcorno, Carlo. "Rassegna di studi sulla predicazione medievale e umanistica (1970-1980)." *Lettere italiane* 33 (1981): 235-76.

789

Dieter, Otto A.L. "*Arbor picta*: The Medieval Tree of Preaching." *QJS* 51 (1965): 123-44.

790

Evans, Gillian R. and David L. d'Avray. "Unusual 'Ars Praedicandi.'" *Medium Aevum* 49 (1980): 26-31.

791

Forni, A. "Kerygma e adattamento: Aspetti della predicazione cattolica nei secoli XII-XIV." *Bulletino dell'istituto storico italiano per il medio evo e Archivio Muratoriano* 89 (1980-81): 261-348.

792

Gallick, Susan. "*Artes praedicandi*: Early Printed Editions." *MS* 39 (1977): 477-489.

> *Traces thirteen authors through early period of printing (1475-c.1600), finding some (e.g. Basevorn, Higden, Waleys) had no print editions while "pseudo-Aquinas" had the most (18).*

793
Gatch, Milton McC. *Preaching and Theology in Anglo-Saxon England: Aelfric and Wulfstan.* (University of Toronto Press, 1977).
While this book concentrates more on homiletic subject matter than on the form of preaching, it can provide useful insights into the compositional skills of the two preachers in the title.

794
Godet, Jean-François. "Le rôle de la prédication dans l'évolution de l'ordre des Frères Mineurs d'après les écrits de saint François." *Franziskanische Studien* 59 (1977): 53-64.

795
Hinnebusch, William A. *Early English Friars Preachers.* Institutum historicum FF, Praedicatorum Romae ad S. Sabinae, Dissertationes historicae 14. (Rome, 1951).

796
Kerr, Hugh T. *Preaching in the Early Church.* (New York, 1942).

797
Leclercq, Jean. "Le Magistère du prédicateur au XIIIᵉ siècle." *AHDLMA* 15 (1946): 105-47.
This perceptive study includes a brief statement (pp. 108-14) of the "ideal" of the medieval preacher.

798
Lecoy de la Marche, A. *La Chaire française au moyen âge, spécialement au XIIIᵉ siècle.* (Paris, 1886).

799
Letson, D.R. "Form of the Old English Homily." *American Benedictine Review* 30 (1979): 399-431.

800
Little, Andrew G., and Franz Pelster. *Oxford Theology and Theologians c. AD 1282-1302.* (Oxford, 1934).
For sermons and preachers at the University of Oxford in the years 1290-1293, see part II, 147-215.

801

Lubac, Henri de. *Exégèse médiévale: Les quatre sens de l'Écriture.* 4 vols. (Paris, 1959-1964).

802

McGuire, Michael, and John H. Patton. "Preaching in the Mystic Mode: The Rhetorical Art of Meister Eckhart." *Communication Monographs* 44 (1977): 263-272.

> *Analysis of 23 "authenticated" sermon texts of Eckhart (1260-c. 1329).*

803

Mourin, Louis, ed. *Jean Gerson prédicateur français.* (Brugge, 1952).

804

Mourin, Louis, ed. *Six sermons français inédits de Jean Gerson.* Études de théologie et d'histoire de la spiritualité 8. (Paris, 1946).

> *Mourin includes a useful bibliography of 726 items, with sections on medieval preaching theory,* exempla, *proverbs, style, and related matters, pp. 573-606.*

805

Neale, John M. *Mediaeval Preachers and Mediaeval Preaching.* (London, 1856).

806

Owst, Gerald R. *Literature and Pulpit in Medieval England.* 2nd ed. (Oxford, 1961).

> *This second major work by Owst concentrates on literary form and theme as revealed in English preaching, and may therefore be of lesser interest to students of the preaching process itself. Nevertheless chapter 4 (pp. 149-209) on the* exempla *provides a useful treatment of the rhetorical value of this type of medieval preaching support.*

807

Pantin, William A. *English Church in the Fourteenth Century.* (Cambridge University Press, 1955).

> *Pantin includes some useful background material on medieval preaching.*

808
Petry, Ray C. *No Uncertain Sound: Sermons that shaped the Pulpit Tradition.* (Philadelphia, 1948).
Petry includes translations of representative medieval sermons and indicates that there was no generally accepted theory of preaching prior to the twelfth century.

809
Petry, Ray C. *Preaching in the Great Tradition.* (Philadelphia, 1950).

810
Rambaud, Louis. *L'Eloquence française: la chaire, le barreau, la tribune.* 2 vols. (Lyons, [1948?]).

811
Reinitzer, Heimo, ed. *Beiträge zur Geschichte der Predigt: Vorträge und Abhandlungen.* Vestigia Bibliae 3. (Hamburg, 1981).

812
Rico, Francisco. *Predicación y Litteratura en la España Medieval.* (Cádiz: Universidad Nacional de Educacion a Distancia, Centro Asociado de Cádiz, 1977).

813
Roberts, Phyllis B. *Stephanus de Lingua-Tonante: Studies in the Sermons of Stephen Langton.* Pontifical Institute Studies and Texts, 16. (Toronto, 1968).
An interesting investigation into the relation of theory and practice in sermon-making.

814
Robertson, Durant W., Jr. "Frequency of Preaching in Thirteenth Century England." *Speculum* 24 (1949): 376-388. (Reprinted with addenda in D. W. Robertson. *Essays in Medieval Culture.* Princeton University Press, 1980, pp. 114-128, 351-355.)

815
Robson, Charles A. *Maurice of Sully and the Medieval Vernacular Homily, with the Text of Maurice's French Homilies from a Sens Cathedral Chapter MS.* (Oxford, 1952).

816

Ross, Woodburn O., ed. *Middle English Sermons*. Early English Text Society 209. (London, 1940).
The introduction contains a useful summary of preaching theory.

817

Rusconi, Roberto. *Predicazione e vita religiosa nella società italiana: da Carlo Magno alla Controriforma*. Documenti della Storia, 30. (Turin, 1981).
Presents 162 excerpts from medieval documents relating to preaching. All are translated into Italian.

818

Schneyer, Johann B. *Geschichte der katholischen Predigt*. (Freiburg im Bresgau, 1969).

819

Sedgwick, Walter B. "Origins of the Sermon." *Hibbert Journal* 45 (1947): 158-64.

820

Smalley, Beryl. *English Friars and Antiquity in the Early Fourteenth Century*. (Oxford, 1960).
Some comment on preaching techniques is included in this excellent study of medieval humanism.

821

Smalley, Beryl. "Stephen Langton and the Four Senses of Scripture." *Speculum* 6 (1931): 60-76.
Smalley uses Langton to illustrate the medieval habit of developing the meaning of a text from the multiple senses found in it.

822

Smith, Lucy Toulmin. "English Popular Preaching in the Fourteenth Century." *EHR* 7 (1892): 25-36.

823

Sweet, Jennifer. "Some Thirteenth-Century Sermons and Their Authors." *JEH* 4 (1953): 27-36.
Sweet discusses the use of "theme" and "protheme" by sixteen

preachers.

824

Vicaire, Marie-Humbert. "La prédication nouvelle des prêcheurs méridionaux au XIIIe siècle." In *Dominique et ses prêcheurs.* (Fribourg: Éditions Universitaires de Fribourg-Éditions du Cerf, 1977). Pp. 35-57. (Reprinted from *Cahiers de fanjeaux* 6 [1971]. Pp. 101-32.)

825

Wackernagel, Wilhelm. *Altdeutsche Predigten und Gebete.* (Basel, 1876).

826

Wailes, Stephen L. "Composition of Vernacular Sermons by Berthold von Regensburg." *Michigan Germanic Studies* 5 (1979): 1-24.

A perceptive study of the relation between theory and practice as exemplified in the sermons of Berthold, a Franciscan who died in 1272; includes statistical analyses of organizational patterns in 38 sermons.

827

Wenzel, Siegfried. "Chaucer and the Language of Contemporary Preaching." *Studies in Philology* 73 (1976): 138-61.

828

Wenzel, Siegfried. "Joyous Art of Preaching: or, the Preacher and the Fabliau." *Anglia* 97 (1979): 304-25.

829

Zink, Michel. *La prédication en language romane avant 1300.* (Paris, 1976).

C. Authors and Works

Collections of Texts

830

Caplan, Harry. *Mediaeval Artes praedicandi: A Hand-list.* In *Cornell Studies in Classical Philology 24.* (Ithaca, 1934). (Also *Supplement* [Ithaca, 1936]).

Caplan's two excellent handlists include incipits of unpublished manuscripts, data on published tracts, names of authors arranged by centuries, and a place-inventory of libraries holding manuscripts. For a comparison of the manuscript listings of Caplan and Charland, see Caplan's review of Charland's Artes praedicandi *in* Speculum *13 (1938), 352-4.*

831

Charland, Th.-M. *Artes praedicandi: contribution à l'histoire de la rhétorique au moyen âge.* (Paris and Ottawa: Publications de l'institut d'études médiévales d'Ottawa 7, 1936).

This is an indispensable study in the field, containing an excellent summary of theory, the biographies of known authors, lists of manuscripts, and the Latin texts of treatises of Robert of Basevorn and Thomas Waleys. It is divided into three parts.

Part I (pp. 15-106) contains details on a number of authors and the manuscripts of their work, including the following: Pseudo-Albert the Great, Pseudo-Bonaventure, Francis Ximenes, O.M., Henry of Langenstein (Henry of Hesse), Humbert of Romans, O.P., Jacobus of Fusignano, O.P., Jean of Galles, O.M., Jean of La Rochelle, O.M., Richard of Thetford, Robert of Basevorn, Pseudo-Thomas Aquinas, Thomas Waleys, O.P., William of Auvergne.

Part II (pp. 107-226) deals with preaching theory and its evolution.

Part III (pp. 227-420) includes tables of incipits, proper names, and manuscripts, as well as two important Latin texts:

Robert of Basevorn, Forma praedicandi, *and Thomas Waleys,*
De modo componendi sermones.
[A second edition is now in preparation.]

Alain of Lille: A. Works

832

Evans, Gillian R., trans. *Art of Preaching.* (Kalamazoo, Michigan, 1981).

Translation of Alain's Ars praedicandi, *from the text in PL. In the brief Introduction Evans describes this version as "an English working text," necessary until a critical Latin edition is prepared to replace the "far from satisfactory" Migne text.*

833

Miller, Joseph M., trans. *Compendium on the Art of Preaching.* Preface and Selected Chapters. In *Readings.* Pp. 229-239.

Translation of excerpts from Alain's De arte predicatoria.

834

Summa de arte praedicatoria. In *PL* 210, cols. 110-98.

This treatise, like that of Guibert of Nogent, illustrates the comparatively inchoate nature of preaching theory prior to the emergence of the "thematic" sermon.

Alain of Lille: B. Secondary References

835

d'Alverny, Marie-Thérèse. *Alain de Lille, Textes inédits.* (Paris, 1965).

An excellent survey of Alain's works and career.

836

Evans, Gillian R. *Alan of Lille: The Frontiers of Theology in the Later Twelfth Century.* (Cambridge University Press, 1983).

837

Evans, Gillian R. "Book of Experience: Alain of Lille's Use of the Classical Rhetorical Topos in His Pastoral Writings." *Analecta*

Cisterciensia 32 (1977 for 1976): 113-21.

838

Roussel, H. and F. Suard. *Alain de Lille, Gautier de Châtillon, Jakemart Giélée et leur temps.* (Lille, 1980).

839

Trout, John M. "Alain of Lille and the Art of Preaching in the Twelfth Century." *Bulletin de théologie ancienne et medievale* 12 (1980): 642-653.

Alphonsus Dalprau

840

Hauf, Albert G. "El 'Ars praedicandi' de Fr. Alfonso d'Alprão, O.F.M. Aportación al estudio de la teoría de la predicación en la Península Ibérica." *Archivum Franciscanum Historicum* 72 (1979): 233-329.

Includes the text (pp. 263-329) of Ars praedicandi, conferendi, collationandi, arengandi, secundum multiplicem modum by Alphonsus Dalprau (or d'Alprão) dated 1397 in one manuscript.

Anonymous 'ars praedicandi'

841

Allen, Judson B. "Unrecorded *Ars praedicandi.*" *Wake Forest University Library Newsletter* 1 (1969).

Describes the contents of a treatise, De modo praedicandi, in Wake Forest University Library Ms. 242/En 1.

Bernardino of Siena

842

Delcorno, Carlo. "L''ars praedicandi' di Bernardino da Siena." *Lettere italiane* 32 (1980): 441-75.

Bonaventure (Pseudo-Bonaventure): A. Works

843
Ars concionandi. In *S. Bonaventurae opera omnia 9.* (Quaracchi, 1882-1902). Pp. 8-21.

Bonaventure (Pseudo-Bonaventure): B. Secondary References

844
Hazel, Harry C. "Bonaventuran 'Ars concionandi.'" In *S. Bonaventura, 1274-1974: II, Studia de vita, mente, fontibus et operibus sancti Bonaventurae.* (Rome, 1973). Pp. 435-446.

Concludes that ideas in the Ars concionandi *are consistent with Bonaventure's sermons and other writings, even if the Quaracchi editors are doubtful of the attribution of the work to him.*

845
Piacentini, Ernesto. "La 'Ars concionandi' dello Pseudo-Bonaventura. Importanza, sviluppo e struttura del Sermone Tematico nella predicazione medioevale." *Miscellanea Francescana* 75 (1975): 325-54.

Géraud du Pescher

846
Delorme, Ferdinand. "L'*Ars faciendi sermones* de Géraud du Pescher." *Antonianum* 19 (1944): 169-198.

Includes text of the treatise previously known only in an abridged version attributed to one "Astasius O.F.M."

Guibert de Nogent

847
Miller, Joseph M., trans. *A Book about the Way a Sermon Ought to be Given.* In *Readings.* Pp. 162-181.

Humbert of Romans

848

Treatise on Preaching. Trans. the Dominican Students, Province of St. Joseph. Ed. W.M. Conlon. (Westminster, Maryland, 1951).
Humbert was the second Master General of the "Order of Preachers" (Dominicans).

849

"Treatise On the Formation of Preachers." In *Early Dominicans: Selected Writings.* Ed. and trans. Simon Tugwell O.P. (New York, 1982). Pp. 183-385.
Translation of several sections from Humbert's book of advice for preachers.

John of Rochelle

850

Cantini, P.G., ed. *"Processus negociandi themata sermonum* di Giovanni della Rochelle O.F.M." *Antonianum* 26 (1951): 247-270.

John of Wales

851

Ross, Woodburn O. "Brief *Forma predicandi.*" *Modern Philology* 34 (1937): 337-344.
Includes a shortened version of the text In isto libello *(Caplan Handlist 62)* attributed to John of Wales O.F.M. (d. 1302).

Ramon Llull

852

Wittlin, C., ed. and comm. *Art abreujada de predicació.* Biblioteca Escriny. (Colleccio de Textos Medievals Breus, 4, Sant Broi de Llobregat, 1982).
Edition of a Catalan text (1313) attributed to Llull.

Ranulph Higden: A. Works

853

Jennings, Margaret, ed. Ars Componendi Sermones *of Ranulph Higden O.S.B.: A Critical Edition.* Davis Medieval Texts and Studies, Vol. VI. (Leiden, 1988).

Ranulph Higden: B. Secondary References

854

Jennings, Margaret. "Monks and the *Artes Praedicandi* in the Time of Ranulph Higden: An Acknowledgement." *Revue bénédictine* 87 (1977): 389-90.

855

Jennings, Margaret. "Preacher's Rhetoric: The *Ars componendi sermones* of Ranulph Higden." In *Medieval Eloquence.* Pp. 112-26.

Thomas Chabham

856

Longère, Jean. "Quelques 'Summae de poenitentia' à la fin du XIIe et au début du XIIIe siècle." In *La piété populaire au moyen âge. Actes du 99e Congrès national des Sociétés savantes. Besancon, 1974.* (Paris, 1977). Pp. I, 45-58.

> *Includes a discussion of Thomas Chabham, whose ground-breaking* Summa De arte praedicandi *(c. 1205) combines a pastoral manual and a treatise on how to compose thematic sermons.*

Thomas of Todi

857

Miller, Joseph M., trans. *The Art of Giving Sermons and Preparing Conferences* (Excerpts). In *Readings.* Pp. 273-279.

> *The excerpts are from Babcock's 1941 M.A. thesis.*

William of Auvergne

858

de Poorter, A. "Un manuel de prédication médiévale." *Revue néoscolastique de philosophie* 25 (1923): 192-209.

Includes an edition of the De arte predicandi *of William of Auvergne (Bishop of Paris, 1228-1249).*

D. Exempla, Sermon Collections, and Other Preachers' Aids

859

Bataillon, Louis-Jacques. "Les instruments de travail des prédicateurs au XIIIe siècle." In *Culture et travail intellectuel dans l'Occident médiéval.* (Paris, 1978). Pp. 197-209.

Discusses such older preacher's aids as sermon collections, florilegia, *glosses, and homiliaries, as well as newer ones like concordances, glossaries,* artes praedicandi, *and collections of* exempla *and* distinctiones.

860

Bremond, C., J. LeGoff, and J.-C. Schmitt. *L'Exemplum.* Typologie des sources du Moyen Age occidental, 40. (Turnhout, 1982).

861

D'Avray, David L. "Wordlists in the 'Ars faciendi sermones' of Geraldus de Piscario." *Franciscan Studies* 38 (1978): 184-193.

Notes that the wordlists in Geraldus' text actually form a "dictionary of double rhymes" for preachers wishing to construct rhymed divisions, and sees an explanation of the system in Thomas Waleys' De modo componendi sermones.

862

Geremek, Bronislaw. "L'*exemplum* et la circulation de la culture au moyen âge." *Mélanges de l'école française de Rome* 92 (Paris, 1980): 153-179.

863

Gillespie, Vincent. "*Doctrina* and *Predicacio*: The Design and Function of Some Pastoral Manuals." *Leeds Studies in English*

N.S. 11 (1980): 36-50.

864

McGuire, B.P. "Cistercians and the Rise of the 'Exemplum' in Early Thirteenth Century France: a Reevaluation of Paris B.N. Ms. lat 15912." *Classica et Medievalia* 34 (1983): 211-267.

865

Michaud-Quantin, Pierre. "Guy d'Evreux O. P., Technicien du sermonnaire médiéval." *AFP* 20 (1950): 213-33.

> *Describes a popular Dominican collection of 66 sermons (ca. 1293) characterized by divisions of Theme and Protheme.*

866

Mosher, Joseph A. *The Exemplum in the Early Religious and Didactic Literature of England.* (New York, 1911).

> *This is the best single treatment of* exempla *in English, though Mosher does not adequately handle their use in preaching. See also Welter.*

867

Rouse, Richard H. and Mary A. Rouse. *Preachers, Florilegia and Sermons: Studies on the* Manipulus Florum *of Thomas of Ireland.* (Toronto, 1979).

> *A useful introduction to the variety of kinds of sermon aids available to medieval preachers, as well as a detailed analysis of one particular work.*

868

Tubach, Frederick C. *Index exemplorum: A Handbook of Medieval Religious Tales.* FF Communications, 204. (Helsinki, 1969).

869

Vitale-Brovarone, Alessandro. "Persuasione e narrazione: l'*exemplum* tra due retoriche (VI-XII Sec.)." *Mélanges de l'École Française de Rome. Moyen Âge-temps modernes* 92 (1980): 87-112.

870

von Nolcken, Christina. "Some Alphabetical *Compendia* and How Preachers Used Them in Fourteenth-Century England."

Viator 12 (1981): 271-88.

> *Includes (pp. 280-281) the outline of a model sermon constructed by* distinctiones.

871

Welter, J.-Th. *L'Exemplum dans la littérature religieuse et didactique du moyen âge.* (Paris, 1927).

> *This is probably the best single discussion of* exempla, *though Welter has little regard for rhetorical implications of the genre and consequently misunderstands some aspects of its use in preaching. See also Mosher*

VII
University *Disputation*
and Scholastic Method

Dialectical disputations, or oral debates using syllogistic patterns based on Aristotelian logic, were a feature of at least some medieval schools by the twelfth century. Peter Cantor, a twelfth-century teacher at Paris, declares that disputation is a central obligation of the master: "A teaching master has three duties: to lecture, to preach, and to dispute." And when William Fitzstephen visited London's St. Paul's school in the 1170's he found adolescent boys competing in Latin disputations.

But it was in the universities from the thirteenth century onward that *disputatio* played its most important role, becoming an integral part of the whole teaching and examination process. In the classroom the master's reading and commentary (*lectio*) on a text would lead typically to *quaestiones*, or issues to be resolved by debate (*disputatio*). Ultimately the disputation also came to be the primary form of examination for the student. This basic process was at the core of the so-called "scholastic method" which dominated European universities for centuries. The arts, law, theology, and even medicine were investigated in this manner. The massive *Summa theologica* of Thomas Aquinas, for example, is virtually a written form of the typical classroom process.

Incoming university students were obliged to begin their studies with two Aristotelian works on dialectic—the *De sophisticis elenchis* (*On Sophistical Refutations*) and the *Topica* (*Topics*) whose eighth book includes directions for conducting dialectical disputations with an opposing speaker. Then for three or more years disputation became a central activity for the students. Thus it was that thousands and thousands of university-trained men were exposed to dialectical habits of thought. This experience must surely have had effects on medieval thinking about language, about writing, and about speaking; nevertheless this relation to date is largely unexplored.

872
Bazan, Bernardo C. "La *Quaestio disputata.*" In *Les genres littéraires dans les sources théologiques et philosophiques médiévales: Définition, critique et exploitation.* In *Actes du Colloque international de Louvain, 25-27 mai 1981.* (Louvain, 1982). Pp. 31-49.

> *The most important single brief description of the* disputatio *as a genre of discourse. Bazan treats its evolution, its place in the university, its species, its methods, and its texts.*

873
Bird, Otto. "Formalizing of the Topics in Mediaeval Logic." *Notre Dame Journal of Formal Logic* 1 (1960): 138-149.

874
de Rijk, Lambert Marie. *Die mittelalterlichen Traktate* De modo opponendi et respondendi. *Einleitung und Ausgabe der Einschlägigen Texte.* Beiträge zur Geschichte der Philosophie und Theologie des Mittelalters, Neue Folge, Band. 17. (Münster

Westfalen, 1980).

> *Texts of four treatises dealing with argumentative procedures in dialectical disputation:* Thesaurus philosophorum, *(two versions),* Pseudo-Albertus Magnus De modo opponendi et respondendi, *and Gentilis de Monte Sancte Marie in Georgio,* De arte et modo disputandi.

875
de Rijk, Lambert Marie. *Logica Modernorum: A Contribution to the History of Early Terminist Logic.* 2 vols. (Assen).

> *Vol. I treats Fallacies, Vol. II the theory of Supposition. A useful if complex introduction to the logic underlying medieval disputational practice.*

876
Ehninger, Douglas, and Bromley Smith. "Terrafilial Disputations at Oxford." *QJS* 36 (1950): 333-9.

877
Evans, Gillian R. "'Argumentum' and 'argumentatio': The Development of a Technical Terminology up to c. 1150." *Classical Folia* 30 (1976): 81-93.

878
Gibson, Margaret T. "Latin Commentaries on Logic before 1200." *Bulletin de philosophie médiévale* 24 (1982): 54-64.

879
G[ibson], S[trickland]. "Order of Disputations." *Bodleian Quarterly Record* 6 (1930): 107-12.

880
Glorieux, Palémon. "Aux origines du quodlibet." *Divus Thomas: commentarium de philosophia et theologia* 38 (1935): 502-22.

> *The* quodlibet *was a type of disputation less restrictive in its rules than the ordinary classroom type.*

881
Glorieux, Palémon. *La Littérature quodlibétique de 1260 à 1320.* Bibliothèque thomiste 5 and 21. (Paris, 1925-35).

882

Glorieux, Palémon. *Répertoire des maîtres en théologie de Paris au XIIIe siècle.* Etudes de philosophie médiévale 17-18. 2 vols. (Paris, 1933-4).

The first volume has an excellent brief survey of disputation practices. The biographies of university masters given by Glorieux often list the subjects of their disputations.

883

Gössmann, Elisabeth. "Dialektische und rhetorische Implikationen der Auseinandersetzung zwischen Abaelard und Bernhard von Clairvaux um die Gotteserkenntnis." In *Sprache und Erkenntnis im Mittelalter: Akten des VI. Internationalen kongresses für mittelalterliche Philosophie der Société Internationale pour l'Étude de la Philosophie Médiévale, Bonn, 29 August-3 September 1977.* Ed. W. Kluxen et al. (Berlin-New York, 1981). Vol. II, 890-902.

884

Grabmann, Martin. *Die Geschichte der scholastischen Methode.* 2 vols. (Freiburg in Breisgau, 1909-11). (Reprinted Basel/Stuttgart, [1961].)

This important treatment of the subject, originally published in 1909-11, describes the men and the intellectual developments up to the thirteenth century that led to the so-called scholastic method. Still a major historical survey even after nearly eight decades.

885

Green-Pedersen, Niels J. "On the Interpretation of Aristotle's *Topics* in the Thirteenth Century." *CIMAGL* 9 (1973): 1-46.

886

Green-Pedersen, Niels J. *Tradition of the Topics in the Middle Ages: The Commentaries on Aristotle's and Boethius' 'Topics.'* (Munich, 1984).

This volume first treats the main sources of the medieval doctrine of the topics—Aristotle and Boethius—then takes up the general views of their medieval commentators before turning to a century-by-century survey. While the author specifically limits his discussion to the topics of the logicians, students of rhetoric may find this a useful source for medieval ideas concerning the loci *in general.*

887

Iwakuma, Y., ed. comm. " 'Instantiae' A Study of Twelfth-Century Technique of Argumentation with an Edition of Ms. Paris BN Lat. 6674, f. 1-5." *CIMAGL* 38 (1981): 1-91.

888

Jolivet, Jean. *Arts du langage et théologie chez Abélard.* Études de philosophie mediévale, LVII. (Paris, 1969).

An illuminating discussion of how Abelard's concept of the trivium *influenced his "method of thought." Although Jolivet does not treat rhetoric* per se, *many readers may find in this well-documented book a number of thoughtful insights into twelfth-century concepts of such subjects as dialectic, grammar, argument, word, and proof.*

889

Korolec, Jerzy B. "Jean Buridan et Jean de Jandun et la relation entre la rhétorique et la dialectique." In *Sprache und Erkenntnis im Mittelalter.* Ed. Wolfgang Kluxen et al. Vol. 2. Miscellenea Mediaevalia Band 13/2. Akten der VI. Internationalen Kongresses für mittelalterliche Philosophie der Société Internationale pour l'Étude de la Philosophie Médiévale, 29 August-3 September 1977. (Berlin, 1981). Pp. 622-627.

890

Lewry, P. Osmond. "Rhetoric at Paris and Oxford in the Mid-Thirteenth Century." *Rhetorica* 1 (1983): 45-63.

This detailed study includes heretofore unpublished manuscript material, especially from examination compendia.

891

Murphy, James J. "Two Medieval Textbooks in Debate." *Journal of the American Forensic Association* 1 (1964): 1-6.

This article discusses the role of Aristotle's Topica *and* De sophisticis elenchis *in training university students in* disputatio, *especially after John of Salisbury's praise of the two books in his* Metalogicon *(1149).*

892

Pellegrini, Angelo M. "Renaissance and Medieval Antecedents of Debate." *QJS* 28 (1942): 14-19.

893

Smith, Bromley. "Extracurricular Disputations, 1400-1650." *QJS* 34 (1948): 473-6.

894

Stump, Eleonore. "Topics: Their Development and Absorption into Consequences." In *The Cambridge History of Later Medieval Philosophy from the Rediscovery of Aristotle to the Disintegration of Scholasticism, 1100-1600.* Norman Kretzmann, Anthony Kenny and Jan Pinborg eds. (Cambridge University Press, 1982). Pp. 273-299.

An important discussion of the role of the topics.

895

Stump, Eleonore. "Dialectic." In *The Seven Liberal Arts in the Middle Ages.* Ed. David L. Wagner. (Indiana University Press, 1983). Pp. 125-146.

Concentrates on the eleventh to thirteenth centuries, a period in which "dialectic" is the branch of logic dealing with the discovery of "believable arguments." Discusses the contributions of Boethius, Garlandus Compotista, and Peter of Spain, with special attention to topical invention in the scholastic period.

896

Stump, Eleonore. "Dialectic in the Eleventh and Twelfth Centuries: Garlandus Compotista." *History and Philosophy of Logic* 1 (1980): 1-18.

Discussion of the Dialectica *(before 1040?) of Garlandus Compotista, which Stump describes as "the earliest complete medieval logic still extant." She sees it as a bridge between Boethius and the later scholasticism.*

897
Stump, Eleonore. "William of Sherwood's Treatise on Obligations." *Historiographia linguistica* 7 (1980): 249-64.
Sets medieval treatises on "Obligations" in the context of disputatio.

898
Ueberweg, Friedrich, and B. Geyer. *Grundriss der Geschichte der Philosophie, II: Die patristische und scholastische Philosophie.* (Berlin, 1928).
Chapter 17 deals with scholastic methods and includes (pp. 683ff.) a bibliography of studies on disputation.

899
Wallerand, G. *Les Oeuvres de Siger de Courtrai.* Les philosophes belges: textes et études 8. (Louvain, 1913).
Chapter four deals with "Le procédé pedagogique du 'Sophisma.'"

900
Weisheipl, James A., O.P. "Curriculum of the Faculty of Arts at Oxford in the Early Fourteenth Century." *MS* 26 (1964): 143-85.
Includes a discussion of the role of disputation in teaching at Oxford.

901
Wippel, John F. "Quodlibetal Question as a Distinctive Literary Genre." In *Les genres littéraires dans les sources théologiques et philosophiques médiévales: Définition, critique, et exploitation. Actes du Colloque international de Louvain-la-Neuve, 25-27 Mai, 1981.* (Louvain-la-Neue, 1982). Pp. 67-84.
Discussion of a species of disputed question which came to the fore in the faculty of theology at Paris during the first half of the thirteenth century. Wippel includes critiques of earlier views, such as those of Glorieux and Grabmann.

VIII
Various Sources

902

Aho, James A. "Rhetoric and the Invention of Double Entry Bookkeeping." *Rhetorica* 3 (1985): 21-43.

Argues that Ciceronian and medieval rhetorical ideas underlay the development of bookkeeping methods finally set out by Luca Pacioli.

903

Albertanus of Brescia. *Ars loquendi et tacendi.* Ed. Thor Sundby. In *Brunetto Latinos Levnet og Skrifter.* (Copenhagen, 1869).

Albertanus includes a rhetorical critique of the prayer "Hail Mary."

904

al-Samarqandi, Abu al-Qasim ibn Abi Bakr. *La Samarkandya: petit traité de rhétorique arabe.* Trans. Abderrezzak Lacheref. (Algiers, 1905).

The author's name on the title page is given as Aboulkacem El-Leyth Samarkandi. This is a French translation of an Arabic treatise on metaphor, written c. 1480.

905
Baehr, Rudolf. "Die Rhetorik als Gestaltungsprinzip im Trattato d'Amore Guittones von Arezzo." *Romanische Forschungen* 67 (1956): 320-37.

906
Barakat, Robert A. *Cistercian Sign Language*. (Kalamazoo, Michigan, 1981).
Includes an illustrated dictionary of the signs, together with a history of their development.

907
Bonebakker, Seeger A. "Aspects of the History of Literary Rhetoric and Poetics in Arabic Literature." *Viator* 1 (1970): 75-95.

908
Bonebakker, Seeger A. *Materials for the History of Arabic Rhetoric from the Hilyat al-muha—dara of Ha—timi*. Istituto orientale di Napoli, Annali Suppl. 4. (Naples, 1975).

909
Bruinsma, Henry A. "Chambers of Rhetoric in the History of Dutch Theater." *San Jose Studies* 3 (1977): 38-48.

910
Caplan, Harry. "Memoria: Treasure-House of Eloquence." In *Of Eloquence: Studies in Ancient and Mediaeval Rhetoric*. Ed. and intro. Anne King & Helen North. (Cornell University Press, 1970). Pp. 196-246.

911
Chrétien, J.L. "Le langage des anges selon la scolastique." *Critique* 35 (1979): 674-89. [Part of "Le mythe de la langue universelle," *Critique* 35 (1979), 648-838.].
A survey of five key scholastic writers reveals a consensus that angelic communication is immediate, intuitive, and effective, thus being a type of universal language.

912
Creytens, Raymond. "Le Manuel de conversation de Philippe de Ferrare, O.P. (†1350?)." *AFP* 16 (1946): 107-35.

913
De Rudder, O. "Pour une histoire de la lecture." *Medievales* 3 (1983): 97-110.

914
Di Lorenzo, Raymond D. "Collection Form and the Art of Memory in the *Libellus super Ludo Schachorum* of Jacobus de Cessolis." *MS* 35 (1973): 205-21.
Argues that the exempla *and* sententiae *in the collection are deliberately organized according to the doctrines of artificial memory, including the use of a chess board as a mnemotechnic device.*

915
Evans, Gillian R. "'Probabilis' and 'Proving.'" *ALMA* 42 (1979-80 for 1982): 138-40.

916
Evans, Gillian R. "Similitudes and Signification-Theory in the Twelfth-Century." *The Downside Review* 101 (1983): 306-311.

917
Gehl, Paul. "Mystical Language Models in Monastic Educational Psychology." *Journal of Medieval and Renaissance Studies* 14 (1984): 219-43.
Includes a discussion of the "rhetoric of inexpressibility" as well as the rhetorical and linguistic implications of monastic recitations and monastic silence.

918
Gümpel, K.W. "Musica cum rhetorica: die Handschrift Ripoli 42." *Archiv für Musikwissenschaft* 35 (1978): 57-61.

919
Gundissalinus, Dominicus. *De divisione philosophiae.* Ed. Ludwig Baur. Beiträge zur Geschichte der Philosophie des Mittelalters 4, Heft 2-3. (Münster, 1903). Pp. 1-144.

920
Hajdu, Helga. *Das mnemotechnische Schrifttum des Mittelalters.* (Vienna, 1936).

921
Jaffe, Samuel. "Rhetoric and Ideology in a New History of German Literature." *Modern Philology* 71 (1973-74): 304-24.

922
Jarecki, Walter. *Signa loquendi: Die cluniacensischen Signalisten eingeleitet und herausgegeben.* Saecula Spiritalia, Band 4. (Baden-Baden, 1981).
   Editions of six lists of hand- and finger-signals for communication in cloisters enforcing a rule of silence.

923
Kustas, George L. "Function and Evolution of Byzantine Rhetoric." *Viator* 1 (1970): 55-73.

924
Maguire, Henry. *Art and Eloquence in Byzantium.* (Princeton University Press, 1981).

925
Milanese, G. "Tradizione retorica e tradizione gregoriana." In *Antropologia medievale.* (Geneva, 1984). Pp. 48-75.
   Compares musical and verbal traditions.

926
Monfasani, John. "Byzantine Rhetorical Tradition and the Renaissance." In *Renaissance Eloquence.* Pp. 174-87.

927
Pack, Roger A. "*Ars memorativa* from the Late Middle Ages." *AHDLM* 46 (1979): 221-75.
   Text (pp. 229-67) of a Vienna manuscript copied at Bologna in 1425 from an earlier source. Introduction includes summary of contents (p. 227). Follows Roman doctrine of "places" and "images" with some variations.

928

Reijnders, Harry F., ed. *"Aimericus Ars lectoria."* *Vivarium* 9 (1971), 119-137 and 10 (1972): 41-101, 124-176.
Treatise (1086) on proper pronunciation of Latin. Similar to work of Siguinus (below) which was written 1087-1088. For a comparison of the two works see the review of the Siguinis edition by Berthe M. Marti (Speculum 5 [1981], 196-198).

929

Roberts, M. "Rhetoric and Poetic Imitation in Avitus' [of Vienne] Account of the Crossing of the Red Sea." *Traditio* 39 (1983): 29-80.

930

Rubenstein, N. "Political Rhetoric in the Imperial Chancery during the Twelfth and Thirteenth Centuries." *MAE* 14 (1945): 21-43.

931

Siguinus, Magister. *Magister Siguinus Ars lectoria: Un art de lecture à haute voix du onzième siècle. Edition critique.* Ed. J. Engels, C.H. Kneepkens, and H.F. Reijnders. (Leiden, 1979).

932

Van Deusen, Nancy. "Origins of a Significant Medieval Genre: The Musical 'Trope' up to the Twelfth Century." *Rhetorica* 3 (1985): 245-267.

933

Vansina, Jan. *Oral Tradition: A Study in Historical Methodology.* Trans. H.M. Wright. (Chicago, [1965]).

934

Volkmann, Ludwig. "Ars memorativa." *Jahrbuch der kunsthistorischen Sammlungen in Wien NS* 3 (1929): 111-200.

935

von Grunebaum, Gustave E., ed. *Tenth-Century Document of Arabic Literary Theory and Criticism: The Sections on Poetry of al-Bâqillâni's I'jâz al-Qur'ân.* (Chicago, 1950).

936
Wall, Bernice V. *Medieval Latin Version of Demetrius' De elocutione*. Catholic University of America Studies in Medieval and Renaissance Latin 5. (Washington, 1937).

937
Ward, John O. "Classical Rhetoric and the Writing of History in Medieval and Renaissance Culture." In *European History and Its Historians*. Ed. Frank McGregor and Nicholas Wright. (Adelaide University Union Press, 1977). Pp. 1-10.

938
Yates, Frances A. *Art of Memory*. (London, 1966).

939
Yates, Frances A. "Ciceronian Art of Memory." *Medioevo e rinascimento: studi in onore di Bruno Nardi*. (Florence, 1955).

XI
Renaissance

Sometimes it is possible to learn more about an historical period by seeing what its critics or successors have to say about it. For this reason a number of items are included here which reflect either a modern concern for changes from "medieval" to "Renaissance" or which describe works of the fifteenth century containing conscious elements of change.

940

Alessio, Gian Carlo. "Hec Franciscus de Buiti." *Italia medioevale e umanistica* 24 (1981): 64-122.

941

Altmann, Alexander. "*Ars rhetorica* as Reflected in Some Jewish Figures of the Italian Renaissance." In *Essays in Jewish Intellectual History.* (University Press of New England for Brandeis University Press, 1981). Pp. 97-118.

> *Includes discussion of Judah ben Yehiel Messer Leon, author of* The Honeycomb's Flow.

942
Baldwin, Thomas W. *William Shakspere's Small Latine & Lesse Greeke.* 2 vols. (Urbana, Illinois, 1944).
Baldwin includes several discussions of the rhetorical training popular in Renaissance England.

943
Baxandall, Michael. *Giotto and the Orators: Humanist Observers of Painting in Italy and the Discovery of Pictorial Composition, 1350-1450.* (Oxford, 1971).

944
Buck, August. *Italiensche Dichtunglehren von Mittelalter bis zum Ausgang de Renaissance.* (Tübingen, 1952).

945
Chastellain, George. *Les douze dames de rhétorique.* Ed. Louis Batissier. (Paris, 1838).

946
Farris, Giovanni. "Paideia ed umanesimo nel trattato di retorica del Traversagni." *Atti e memorie della società savonese di storia patria* N.S. 15 (1981): 143-161.

947
Gerlo, Alois. "*Opus de Conscribendis Epistolis* of Erasmus and the Tradition of the Ars Epistolica." In *Classical Influences on European Culture, A.D. 500-1500.* Ed. Robert R. Bolgar. (Cambridge University Press, 1971). Pp. 103-114.

948
Gibson, Margaret. "Collected Works of Priscian: The Printed Editions 1470-1859." *Studi Medievali* NS 3.18.1 (1977): 249-60.

949
Gilbert, Neal W. *Renaissance Concepts of Method.* (Columbia University Press, 1960).

950

Henderson, Judith Rice. "Defining the Genre of the Letter: Juan Luis Vives' *De conscribendis epistolis.*" *Renaissance and Reformation, Renaissance et Réforme* N.S. 7 (1983): 89-105.

Notes that Vives' work (1536) rejected the medieval ars dictaminis in favor of the letter as a genre separate from the oration.

951

Henderson, Judith Rice. "Erasmus on the Art of Letter-Writing." In *Renaissance Eloquence.* Pp. 331-55.

A useful discussion of Renaissance epistolography and its conscious turning away from medieval dictaminal practices.

952

Howell, Wilbur S. *Logic and Rhetoric in England, 1500-1700.* (Princeton University Press, 1956).

Howell's judgements about the middle ages tend to stress the scholastic tradition with little attention to other aspects, but the book offers a clear exposition of post-medieval developments.

953

Kauffmann, Georg. "Humanitas und Rhetorik in der deutschen Kunst um 1500." In *L'Humanisme Allemand (1480-1540). XVIIIe Colloque international de Tours.* Ed. Joel Lefebvre and J.-C. Margolin. (Munich, 1979). Pp. 493-504.

954

Kristeller, Paul O. "Philosophy and Rhetoric from Antiquity to the Renaissance." Part five in Kristeller, *Renaissance Thought and Its Sources.* Ed. Michael Mooney. (Columbia University Press, 1979).

Includes a succinct overview of Kristeller's views, including his interest in secular oratory of the middle ages. His extensive notes are valuable in themselves.

955
Kristeller, Paul O. *Renaissance Thought: The Classic, Scholastic, and Humanistic Strains.* (New York, 1961).

956
Mendenhall, John C. *Aureate Terms: A Study in the Literary Diction of the Fifteenth Century.* (Lancaster, Pennsylvania, 1919).

957
Monfasani, John. *George of Trebizond: A Biography and a Study of His Rhetoric and Logic.* (Leiden, 1976).

> *Important study of Georgius Trapezuntius (1395-1486), who moved to Venice about 1417 and spent the rest of his life in Italy. Trapezuntius was influential in bringing Byzantine and other Greek rhetorical ideas to the attention of fifteenth century humanists.*

958
Monfasani, John. "Humanism and Rhetoric." In *Renaissance Humanism: Foundation, Forms, and Legacy.* Ed. Albert Rabil, Jr. Vol. 3 of *Humanism and the Disciplines.* (University of Pennsylvania Press, 1988). Pp. 171-235.

> *The best treatment of the subject to date. Declares (p. 172) that "many humanists rejected the theoretical structure of classical rhetoric and returned to a medieval understanding of the purposes and content of the art."*

959
Pearsall, Derek. "Texts, Textual Criticism, and Fifteenth Century Manuscript Production." In *Fifteenth Century Studies: Recent Essays.* Ed. Robert F. Yeager. (Hamden, Connecticut, 1984). Pp. 122-136.

960
Percival, W. Keith. "Grammar and Rhetoric in the Renaissance." In *Renaissance Eloquence.* Pp. 303-30.

> *Points out that re-discovery of long-lost ancient grammatical treatises, coupled with attacks on medieval scholasticism, led to a rapid rejection of medieval grammatical theories.*

961

Ruysscharert, José. "Lorenzo Guglielmo Traversagni de Savone (1425-1503), un humaniste franciscain oublié." *Archivum franciscanum historicum* 46 (1953): 193-210.

962

Seigel, Jerrold. *Rhetoric and Philosophy in Renaissance Humanism: The Union of Eloquence and Wisdom, Petrarch to Valla.* (Princeton University Press, 1968).

> *While this book may have little of direct value to the student of medieval rhetoric, it discusses the role of humanism and Ciceronian rhetoric in the careers of four Italians: Valla, Petrarch, Salutati, and Bruni.*

963

Struever, Nancy S. *Language of History in the Renaissance. Rhetoric and Historical Consciousness in Florentine Humanism.* (Princeton University Press, 1970).

> *A useful and much-cited discussion of the transition from 'medieval' to 'renaissance' ways of thought.*

964

Trapp, Joseph B. "Rhetoric and the Renaissance." In *Background to the English Renaissance.* Intro. Lectures with Foreword by J. B. Trapp. (London, 1974). Pp. 90-108.

965

Traversagnus de Saona, Gulielmus. *Epitome Margarite Castigate Eloquentie.* Ed. and trans. Ronald H. Martin. (Leeds, 1986).

> *Traversagnus, an Italian Franciscan lecturing in theology at Cambridge University in the 1470's, employed first William Caxton and then the St. Alban's printer to produce copies of his* Margarita *to use in his teaching, then had Caxton publish this epitome of the larger work after leaving Cambridge. The* Margarita *and the* Epitome *combine classical, medieval, and Renaissance concepts of rhetoric.*

966
Traversagnus de Saona, Gulielmus. *Margarita eloquentiae.* Ed. Giovanni Farris. (Savona, 1978).

967
Victor, J.M. "Revival of Llullism at Paris, 1499-1516." *Renaissance Quarterly* 28 (1975): 504-34.
> *Includes a brief discussion of the* Ars *Rhetorica mistakenly attributed to the thirteenth century Franciscan mystic and cabalist.*

968
Ward, John O. "Renaissance Commentators on Ciceronian Rhetoric." In *Renaissance Eloquence.* Pp. 126-187.
> *A continuation of Ward's detailed studies of medieval and Renaissance commentaries.*

969
Welzig, Werner, ed. *Predigt und soziale Wirklichkeit: Beiträge zur Erforschung der Predigtliteratur.* (Amsterdam, 1981).
> *Six essays on preaching in early modern Germany, Hungary, and Italy.*

970
Witt, Ronald. "Medieval 'Ars dictaminis' and the Beginnings of Humanism: a New Construction of the Problem." *Renaissance Quarterly* 35 (1982): 1-35.
> *An extremely important article which analyzes issues in both the medieval and Renaissance phases of rhetoric. Witt makes valuable observations concerning the relations between grammar, rhetoric, eloquence, notarial art,* dictatores, *poetics, civic ideals, and humanism. Suggests a modification of Kristeller's views on the role of* dictatores *in the development of humanism.*

971
Witt, Ronald. "Medieval Italian Culture and the Origins of Humanism." In *Renaissance Humanism: Foundations, Forms, and Legacy.* Ed. E. Rabil. 3 vols. (Philadephia, 1988).

Appendix

A Basic Library for a Study
of Medieval Rhetoric

The following forty items are basic works useful for initiating study in the various fields associated with medieval theories of discourse. The reader is cautioned, however, that a great deal of recent investigation of medieval rhetoric appears in journal articles rather than in books. The reader can best locate these key studies through the annotations for the articles in each section.

Alcuin. *Rhetoric of Alcuin and Charlemagne.* Ed. and trans. Wilbur S. Howell. (Princeton University Press, 1941).

Alexander of Villa Dei. *Das Doctrinale des Alexander de Villa-Dei.* Ed. Dietrich Reichling. In *Monumenta germaniae paedagogica 12.* (Berlin, 1893).

Atkins, John W.H. *English Literary Criticism: The Medieval Phase.* (Cambridge University Press, 1943). (Reprinted London, 1952.)

Augustine of Hippo. *On Christian Doctrine.* Trans. Durant W. Robertson, Jr. Library of Liberal Arts 80. (New York, 1958).

Baldwin, Charles S. *Medieval Rhetoric and Poetic.* (New York, 1928).

Cassiodorus. *An Introduction to Divine and Human Readings.* Trans. Leslie Webber Jones. (Columbia University Press, 1946).

Charland, Th.-M. *Artes praedicandi: contribution à l'histoire de la rhétorique au moyen âge.* (Paris and Ottawa: Publications de l'institut d'études médiévales d'Ottawa 7, 1936).

Cobban, A.B. *Medieval Universities: Their Development and Organization.* (London, 1975).

Curtius, Ernst R. *European Literature and the Latin Middle Ages.* Trans. Willard R. Trask. Bollingen Series 36. (New York, 1953).

Dargan, Edwin C. *History of Preaching.* 2 vols. (New York, 1905). (Reprinted in one volume, 1954.)

Evrard of Béthune. *Eberhardi Bethuniensis Graecismus.* Ed. Ioh. Wrobel. Corpus grammaticorum medii aevi 1. (Wratislava, 1887).

Faral, Edmond. *Les arts poétiques du XIIe et du XIIIe siècle.* Bibliothèque de l'école des hautes études, fascicule 238. (Paris, 1924). (Reprinted Paris, 1958.)

Geoffrey of Vinsauf. *Poetria nova.* Trans. Margaret F. Nims. (Toronto, 1967).

Gervais of Melkley. *Ars poetica.* Kritische ausgabe von Hans-Jürgen Gräbener. Forschungen zur romanischen Philologie, 17. (Münster Westfalen, 1965).

Holtz, Louis. *Donat et la tradition de l'enseignement grammatical: Étude sur l'"Ars Donati" et sa diffusion (IVᵉ-IXᵉ siècles) et édition critique.* Documents, études et répertoires. Publiés par l'Institut de Recherche et d'Histoire des Textes. (Paris, 1981).

Isidore of Seville. *Etymologiarum sive originum libri XX.* Ed. Wallace M. Lindsay. 2 vols. (Oxford, 1911). (Reprinted Oxford, 1985.)

John of Garland. *Parisiana Poetria.* Ed. and trans. Traugott F. Lawler. (Yale University Press, 1974).

John of Salisbury. *Metalogicon.* Trans. Daniel D. McGarry. (University of California Press, 1955).

Kennedy, George A. *Classical Rhetoric and Its Christian and Secular Tradition from Ancient to Modern Times.* (University of North Carolina Press, 1980).

Leff, Gordon. *Paris and Oxford Universities in the Thirteenth and Fourteenth Centuries: An Institutional and Intellectual History.* (New York, 1968).

Longère, Jean. *La prédication médiévale.* (Paris, 1983).

Martianus Capella. *The Marriage of Philology and Mercury.* Trans. William Harris Stahl and Richard Johnson, with E.L. Burge. Vol. 2 of *Martianus Capella and the Seven Liberal Arts.* 2 vols. (Columbia University Press, 1977).

Matthew of Vendôme. *The Art of Versification.* Trans. Aubrey E. Galyon. (Iowa State Univ. Press, 1980).

Miller, Joseph M., Michael H. Prosser, and Thomas W. Benson, eds. *Readings in Medieval Rhetoric.* (Indiana University Press, 1973).

Mosher, Joseph A. *The Exemplum in the Early Religious and Didactic Literature of England.* (New York, 1911).

Murphy, James J., ed. *Medieval Eloquence: Studies in the Theory and Practice of Medieval Rhetoric.* (University of California Press, 1978).

Murphy, James J. "Middle Ages." In *The Present State of Scholarship in Historical and Contemporary Rhetoric.* Ed. Winifred Bryan Horner. (University of Missouri Press, 1983). Pp. 40-74.

Murphy, James J. *Rhetoric in the Middle Ages: A History of Rhetorical Theory from Saint Augustine to the Renaissance.* (University of California Press, 1974, 1981).

Murphy, James J., ed. *Renaissance Eloquence: Studies in the Theory and Practice of Renaissance Rhetoric.* (University of California Press, 1983).

Murphy, James J., ed. *Three Medieval Rhetorical Arts.* (University of California Press, 1971).

Owst, Gerald R. *Literature and Pulpit in Medieval England.* 2nd ed. (Oxford, 1961).

Owst, Gerald R. *Preaching in Medieval England: An Introduction to Sermon Manuscripts of the Period, c. 1350-1450.* (Cambridge University Press, 1926). (Reprinted New York, 1965.)

Paetow, Louis J. *Arts Course at Medieval Universities with Special Reference to Grammar and Rhetoric.* (Champaign, Illinois, 1910).

Rashdall, Hastings. *Universities of Europe in the Middle Ages.* Ed. F.M. Powicke and A.B. Emden. 3 vols. (Oxford University Press, 1936).

Reinsma, Luke M. "Middle Ages." In *Historical Rhetoric: An Annotated Bibliography of Sources in English.* Ed. Winifred Bryan Horner. (Boston, 1980). Pp. 45-108.

Robins, Robert H. *Ancient and Medieval Grammatical Theory in Europe.* (London, 1951; rpt. New York, 1971).

Rockinger, Ludwig. *Briefsteller und Formelbücher des eilften bis vierzehnten Jahrhunderts.* Quellen und Erörterungen zur bayerischen und deutschen Geschichte 9. (Munich, 1863). (Reprinted in two volumes with continuous pagination, New York, 1961.)

Thurot, Charles. "Notices et extraits de divers manuscrits latins pour servir à l'histoire des doctrines grammaticales au moyen âge." *Notices et extraits* 22 (1868): 1-592. (Reprinted Frankfurt-am-Main, 1964.)

Wagner, David L. "Seven Liberal Arts and Classical Scholarship." In *The Seven Liberal Arts in the Middle Ages.* Ed. David L. Wagner. (Indiana University Press, 1983). Pp. 1-31.

Woods, Marjorie Curry, ed. and trans. *Early Commentary on the 'Poetria nova' of Geoffrey of Vinsauf.* (New York, 1985).

Index